on

D0469289

Very Short Introductions available now:

ADVERTISING Winston Fletcher

AFRICAN HISTORY
    John Parker and Richard Rathbone

AMERICAN POLITICAL PARTIES
    AND ELECTIONS L. Sandy Maisel

THE AMERICAN
    PRESIDENCY Charles O. Jones

ANARCHISM Colin Ward

ANCIENT EGYPT Ian Shaw

ANCIENT PHILOSOPHY Julia Annas

ANCIENT WARFARE
    Harry Sidebottom

ANGLICANISM Mark Chapman

THE ANGLO-SAXON AGE John Blair

ANIMAL RIGHTS David DeGrazia

ANTISEMITISM Steven Beller

THE APOCRYPHAL GOSPELS
    Paul Foster

ARCHAEOLOGY Paul Bahn

ARCHITECTURE Andrew Ballantyne

ARISTOTLE Jonathan Barnes

ART HISTORY Dana Arnold

ART THEORY Cynthia Freeland

ATHEISM Julian Baggini

AUGUSTINE Henry Chadwick

AUTISM Uta Frith

BARTHES Jonathan Culler

BESTSELLERS John Sutherland

THE BIBLE John Riches

BIBLICAL ARCHEOLOGY Eric H. Cline

BIOGRAPHY Hermione Lee

THE BOOK OF MORMON
    Terryl Givens

THE BRAIN Michael O'Shea

BRITISH POLITICS Anthony Wright

BUDDHA Michael Carrithers

BUDDHISM Damien Keown

BUDDHIST ETHICS Damien Keown

CAPITALISM James Fulcher

CATHOLICISM Gerald O'Collins

THE CELTS Barry Cunliffe

CHAOS Leonard Smith

CHOICE THEORY Michael Allingham

CHRISTIAN ART Beth Williamson

CHRISTIAN ETHICS D. Stephen Long

CHRISTIANITY Linda Woodhead

CITIZENSHIP Richard Bellamy

CLASSICAL MYTHOLOGY
    Helen Morales

CLASSICS
    Mary Beard and John Henderson

CLAUSEWITZ Michael Howard

THE COLD WAR Robert McMahon

COMMUNISM Leslie Holmes

CONSCIOUSNESS Susan Blackmore

CONTEMPORARY ART
    Julian Stallabrass

CONTINENTAL
    PHILOSOPHY Simon Critchley

COSMOLOGY Peter Coles

THE CRUSADES Christopher Tyerman

CRYPTOGRAPHY
    Fred Piper and Sean Murphy

DADA AND SURREALISM
    David Hopkins

DARWIN Jonathan Howard

THE DEAD SEA SCROLLS
    Timothy Lim

DEMOCRACY Bernard Crick

DESCARTES Tom Sorell

DESERTS Nick Middleton

DESIGN John Heskett

DINOSAURS David Norman

DIPLOMACY Joseph M. Siracusa

DOCUMENTARY FILM
    Patricia Aufderheide

THE VIKINGS Julian Richards
WITCHCRAFT Malcolm Gaskill
WITTGENSTEIN A. C. Grayling
WORLD MUSIC
  Philip Bohlman

THE WORLD TRADE
  ORGANIZATION
  Amrita Narlikar
WRITING AND SCRIPT
  Andrew Robinson

AVAILABLE SOON:

NUMBERS Peter M. Higgins
ROMANTICISM Michael Ferber
UTOPIANISM Lyman Sargent

THE BLUES Elijah Wald
ENGLISH LITERATURE
  Jonathan Bate

For more information visit our web site
www.oup.co.uk/general/vsi/

Donald A. Ritchie

# THE U.S. CONGRESS

## A Very Short Introduction

# OXFORD
UNIVERSITY PRESS

Oxford University Press, Inc., publishes works that further
Oxford University's objective of excellence
in research, scholarship, and education.

Oxford  New York
Auckland  Cape Town  Dar es Salaam  Hong Kong  Karachi
Kuala Lumpur  Madrid  Melbourne  Mexico City  Nairobi
New Delhi  Shanghai  Taipei  Toronto

With offices in
Argentina  Austria  Brazil  Chile  Czech Republic  France  Greece
Guatemala  Hungary  Italy  Japan  Poland  Portugal  Singapore
South Korea  Switzerland  Thailand  Turkey  Ukraine  Vietnam

Copyright © 2010 by Donald A. Ritchie

Published by Oxford University Press, Inc.
198 Madison Avenue, New York, NY 10016

www.oup.com

Oxford is a registered trademark of Oxford University Press

Library of Congress Cataloging-in-Publication Data
Ritchie, Donald A., 1945–
The U.S. Congress : a very short introduction / Donald A. Ritchie.
p.  cm. — (Very short introductions)
Includes bibliographical references and index.
ISBN 978-0-19-533831-7 (pbk.)
1. United States. Congress.  I. Title.
II. Title: United States Congress.
JK1041.R58 2010
328.73—dc22
2010013558

1 3 5 7 9 8 6 4 2

Printed in Great Britain
by Ashford Colour Press Ltd., Gosport, Hants.
on acid-free paper

# Acknowledgments

While I view Congress from the Senate side of the Capitol, I have benefited from the thoughtful observations of two specialists on the House, Kenneth Kato of the Center for Legislative Archives at the National Archives, and Matthew Wasniewski of the House Office of History and Preservation, and only wish that there had been space to incorporate all of their suggestions. Rodney Joseph, a friend and fellow historian, provided a fresh perspective from away from Capitol Hill. Nancy Toff is an astute editor whose advice has long guided my thinking and sharpened my prose. At home, my wife, Anne Ritchie, has been my steady source of encouragement and good counsel. I have dedicated this book to all of my colleagues in the Senate Historical Office, each of whom has helped make the job such a positive learning experience.

# Contents

# List of illustrations

# Preface

Taking its name from the Latin for "coming together," Congress is the place where elected officials from all parts of the United States converge to govern. That coming together can be heard in the many regional accents of its members in debate, their constant references to their home states, and their efforts to protect and promote constituent views and interests in the legislation they enact.

But Congress really does not exist as an institution. The term encompasses both the Senate and the House of Representatives, each operating under different rules and in different atmospheres. Each has its own leadership and its own side of the Capitol Building, where the room numbers are prefixed with either H- or S-. The House and Senate must each pass bills in precisely the same language to send them to the president, and each needs a two-thirds vote to override a veto. They meet jointly to hear the president's State of the Union message, and they hold conference committees to work out differences in the bills they have passed, but otherwise each has little to do with the "other body."

Representatives are also called congressmen and congresswomen, while senators are always senators, but it is misleading to refer to the House alone as Congress, and there is no "Speaker of Congress." When the Constitution says that "Congress shall have power to..." or "Congress may by law..." or "the consent of Congress," it gives that power and responsibility jointly to the House and Senate. Neither body can make a law or appropriate funds on its own.

The term Congress also refers to the legislative sessions conducted during the two years between congressional elections. A Congress is generally divided into two sessions, one each year (occasional emergencies have required a third session of a Congress). Under the Twentieth Amendment to the Constitution, since 1934 sessions of Congress begin on January 3, although the date may vary according to legislative needs. This very short introduction, like all studies of the national legislature, uses "Congress" to identify the two houses together, while regularly drawing distinctions between the rules, powers, and personalities of the House and Senate. Although I have spent my whole professional career on Capitol Hill, I intend the book to be neither a defense nor an apology, but an analysis of how Congress works, how it has changed, and how it relates to the voters, the states, and the other branches of the federal government.

The book highlights, in condensed form, the precedents and practices of the House and Senate, examines how their committees handle legislative business, and observes how their floor proceedings operate to produce laws. It weighs the competition between the legislative branch and the executive and judiciary. The Constitution did not so much divide power between these branches as it forced them to share it, each wanting a larger share. In this struggle, the House and Senate have retained their original constitutional construction and powers while contending with an executive that has grown exponentially in size, influence, and power. Any understanding of Congress will also require a look at how members get elected, what it takes to get reelected, and the nature of representation. Finally, the Capitol provides such an imposing physical setting for Congress, and houses so diverse a cast of characters, that this survey will conclude with a group portrait—a snapshot really—of Capitol Hill.

Based on political history and political science, this book is essentially a tour of Capitol Hill that along the way will point out many of the players, the reasons behind their legislative behavior, the meaning of their parliamentary language, and the evolution of their practices. A good tour should be entertaining as well as educational, incorporating humor and irony without resorting to cynicism. And like any tour, there will not be opportunity to see everything, so it will focus on a few examples, processes, events, and locations, allude to others, and recommend sources for more detail.

# Chapter 1
# The great compromise

Appropriately, Congress began with a compromise. Meeting in Philadelphia in 1787, the constitutional convention crafted a federal government divided into legislative, executive, and judicial branches, and further divided Congress into two houses, believing that a separation of powers would serve as a check against potential tyranny, including the tyranny of a political majority. "Ambition must be made to counteract ambition," James Madison reasoned, anticipating that each branch would guard its own prerogatives jealously, preventing an undue concentration of power. But a standoff developed over the issue of representation in the legislature. Delegates from the larger states wanted both houses of the Congress to reflect the size of a state's population: more people deserved more representation. The smaller states refused to accept any government in which they were not equal to the larger ones.

At this impasse, the convention recessed for the July 4 celebration and appointed a committee to find a solution. The committee split the difference in the "Great Compromise," which set proportional representation in the House of Representatives and equality of the states in the Senate. State delegations in the House would vary in size, while every state would have two senators (Article I, sections 2 and 3). No state could lose its equal standing in the Senate without its consent, which none would ever give. There remained other issues to settle, most significantly how to count enslaved African Americans for purposes of representation and taxation, but without the Great Compromise the rest of the Constitution would have been moot.

What kind of legislative bodies did the Great Compromise create? After the 2000 election, California, the largest state with 35 million residents, sent fifty-three members to the House. The half-million residents of Wyoming, by contrast, rate only a single representative, yet Wyoming and California both elect two senators. This lopsided equation gives states with small populations a big advantage in the Senate. The ten states containing half the people in the United States are represented by 236 of the 435 members to the House, but only twenty senators. The forty states with the other half of the population have eighty senators.

The Constitution set a minimum of thirty thousand inhabitants in each congressional district, but no maximum. After each census, every ten years, the House is reapportioned to reflect changes in population. Beginning with 65 members, it grew steadily until it reached 435 after the 1910 census. The House chamber became so crowded that the members' desks had to be replaced with theater seating. Concerned that anything larger would make the legislative process unwieldy, Congress capped House membership at 435. After every census, some states would then gain seats and others lose them. For years, rural districts fought to prevent losing representatives, which resulted in a great disparity in district size. The longtime House Speaker Sam Rayburn (D-Texas), for instance, had only a third as many people in his rural district as did the representative from Dallas. Not until 1964 did the Supreme Court apply a "one person, one vote" standard to House reapportionment, requiring districts with equal numbers of inhabitants.

Each house of Congress can write its own rules, and the two bodies have evolved differently to accommodate their dissimilar representation. Since the late nineteenth century, the larger House has adopted rules that allowed the majority party to prevail, so long as its members hold together when they vote. The Senate's rules gave greater voice to the minority, whether the minority party, a faction of the majority party, or even a single senator. The House grew hierarchical, while the Senate became a body of equals. Despite their vast differences, however, no bill can become law until both houses pass it with exactly the same wording, down to the last semicolon.

## Why not a parliament?

Some of the ideas discarded at the constitutional convention might have created a legislative branch closer to a parliament, where the prime minister and cabinet secretaries are members of the legislature. Congress might have elected presidents and might have been able to remove them for "maladministration," provisions that could have turned the presidency into something closer to a prime minister, with tenure dependent on retaining the majority in Congress. There were even suggestions that senators serve for life, at no pay, making the Senate a House of Lords, with the House of Representatives as the House of Commons.

Nevertheless, Congress did follow the British Parliament's bicameral model. For more than a century, colonial legislatures had generally been divided between an upper house, or governor's council, and a popularly elected assembly. During the American Revolution, some of the states abolished their upper houses, regarding single-body legislatures as more egalitarian. The Continental Congress and the Congress under the Articles of Confederation were also single bodies. Property holders, however, worried that unchecked democratic legislatures would turn confiscatory, and that way of thinking added extra layers to the Constitution. Whereas representatives would be directly elected by people, senators initially would be elected by the state legislatures, and the Electoral College would choose the president, forming a mixed government to prevent an "excess of democracy."

The U.S. government distinctly differs from parliamentary democracies. Neither the president nor the cabinet secretaries sit in Congress, and no member of any branch can serve simultaneously in another (except for the vice president, whom the Constitution installed as president of the Senate to keep him occupied until and unless he was needed to fill a vacancy in the presidency). Unlike prime ministers, American presidents do not lose office if their party's majority falls in the next congressional elections. So presidents have frequently had to contend with congressional majorities led by the opposition.

The BBC correspondent Alistair Cooke observed that British ambassadors to the United States were invariably puzzled about why there was no "question period" where Congress could quiz presidents on current policies the way the House of Commons questions prime ministers. Cooke explained to them that while separation of the branches prevented this, Congress had the advantage of being able to call the president's cabinet for scrutiny before its committees. He argued that the questions and guffaws that prime ministers and cabinet officers faced in the British House of Commons could not be compared, "as a form of executive torture, to an all-day inquisition by a standing committee of Congress." Without the support of a parliamentary majority, the prime minister's government falls, but congressional majorities can ignore the president's legislative proposals, reject his budget, refuse to confirm his nominees, and decline to approve treaties his administration has negotiated.

Party discipline in Congress ebbs and flows over time, and varies between the House and Senate, but in general it is rarely as strong as in a parliamentary system. Senators and representatives hold themselves accountable first and foremost to their constituents. Party leaders have trouble retaliating against dissidents whose votes they will be courting on the next issue. The majority leader may need to appeal to members of the opposition to win a vote. Conversely, congressional leaders rarely need worry about third parties or forge coalitions to govern, as happens in parliamentary systems, since none of the states practice proportional representation to help smaller parties gain seats in Congress. Even the physical setting differs. Unlike most parliaments, where the major parties hector each other while directly facing each other, the semicircular seating in the House and Senate chambers facilitates, at times, bipartisan alliances.

Other democracies overwhelmingly prefer a parliamentary system. The U.S. Congress, by contrast, is slower, more cumbersome, and less efficient—but that was what the framers of the Constitution intended. They designed a system to resist hasty action and temper any sudden shifts in public opinion, to prevent undue concentration of power, to protect citizens' rights, and to forge a national consensus on demanding issues.

## All laws necessary and proper

The Constitution assigns "all legislative powers" to the Congress, together with a long list of specific responsibilities and prohibitions. It implies even more extensive powers by authorizing Congress to make all laws "necessary and proper for carrying into execution the foregoing powers" (Article I, section 8). Known as the "elastic clause," this provision enables Congress to stretch its control over a myriad of new issues without the need for many new constitutional amendments.

Congress has the "power of purse," the sole right to appropriate funds for all federal spending and the burden of raising revenue to pay for it. The Constitution's "commerce clause" gives Congress authority to regulate commerce between the states, and between the United States and other nations (Article I, section 8). Laws setting minimum wages and maximum hours of work in the 1930s came about under the commerce clause, as did the outlawing of racial segregation in the 1960s. Congress has the power to set up the federal court system and set the number of justices on the Supreme Court. It can coin money and borrow it, authorize post offices, build post roads, regulate immigration, and to write laws for bankruptcy and copyright (Article I, section 8). By two-thirds majorities, Congress can send constitutional amendments to the states for approval (Article V).

Congressional influence over foreign and military policy is more ambiguous. Congress has the authority to raise an army and a navy, fund the national defense, and declare war (Article I, section 8), though modern presidents have made expansive claims of authority under their title as commander in chief of the armed services (Article II, section 2). The nation has repeatedly gone into combat without formal declarations of war, and war-making powers have become the greatest area of contention between the branches of the government.

Contrary to orderly flow charts designed to show how a bill becomes law, legislation often follows a convoluted path through Congress. Many initiatives are bundled into enormous legislative packages, a tactic that requires supporters and opponents to swallow more than they might otherwise. Bundling further heightens tension between the Congress and the president, who must sign or veto these "omnibus" bills. By the time most bills reach the president's desk, they have acquired so much support, making it hard for him to reject them without suffering adverse political consequences.

Buffeted by opposing factions, lawmakers constantly make difficult choices. No single member can push a major bill through Congress unchanged; nor can presidents expect to get everything they want, except under dire circumstances. At the depth of the Depression, Franklin D. Roosevelt submitted an emergency banking bill that the House passed that same morning, the Senate passed that afternoon, and Roosevelt signed that evening. No one in Congress had time to read the entire bill. They voted it into law out of desperation, and fortunately it worked to restore public confidence in the banking system. In a similar rush, within a week after the terrorist attacks on September 11, 2001, Congress passed the USA PATRIOT Act (HR 3162), knowing that the public expected a speedy, bipartisan response. After some time had elapsed, however, there were those who wished that Congress had given more consideration to its provisions affecting civil liberties. Most bills take much longer, since they must leap hurdles in two houses that are widely disparate in structure, procedure, and discipline.

## The people's house

At each meeting of the House of Representatives, its sergeant at arms carries into the chamber the House mace, a forty-inch silver shaft topped by an American eagle, a design derived from ancient Rome, via the British Parliament. The mace is placed on a pedestal beside the Speaker's rostrum to indicate that the House is in regular session. When the House acts as a committee of the whole, to relax its rules and expedite business, the mace is set on a lower pedestal to indicate the shift. If tempers flare and disturbances erupt, the sergeant at arms restores order by lifting the mace high as a symbol of the dignity of the House. The smaller, more sedate Senate has never found the need for a mace.

The House now consists of 435 representatives, a resident commissioner from the Commonwealth of Puerto Rico, and five delegates from the territories and the District of Columbia. Delegates can vote in the committees but not on the House floor. Like most state legislatures, representatives vote by an electronic voting system, inserting a card into one of the forty-six voting boxes throughout the chamber, and pressing yes, no, or present. A large illuminated scoreboard above the gallery shows a green light for those who voted aye, red for nay, and amber for present.

Over the side entrances, electronic tallies indicate the number of votes cast for and against the bill, and the amount of time left to vote. Members stream in and mill about the floor in animated knots, cheering on their side's vote count. Even during debate the House seems to be in constant movement. Members rise to deliver short, often sharp speeches from podiums in the well at the front of the chamber, while the bill's managers sit at tables equipped with microphones to enable them to be heard above the hubbub.

In search of democracy in America, the French political observer Alexis de Tocqueville visited the House in 1832, and he was appalled by the coarse nature of its debate. He assumed that the House represented the lower classes. In the Senate gallery, he listened to dignified orations delivered to attentive members, and he decided this was the American aristocracy. Missouri's Thomas Hart Benton, who served in both the Senate and House, rebutted this interpretation by pointing out that since many senators had previously served in the House, the two bodies did not represent different classes. The larger House has always been louder and busier, more efficient, and more acrimonious than the smaller Senate.

The House evolved into a compound of groups: party conferences, committees, issue caucuses, state delegations, freshman classes, prayer breakfasts, and any other means of creating strength through numbers. The House's three-tiered rostrum aptly symbolizes the structure of the body, from the mass at the bottom to the Speaker at the top. The Speaker began as a neutral presiding officer, modeled after the Speaker in the House of Commons. Once the dynamic, ambitious Henry Clay of Kentucky became Speaker in 1811, however, he made the position more political, so that the Speaker is also leader of the majority party. Using the party conference and behind-the-scenes efforts, the Speaker exerts leadership without voting and usually without participating in floor debates. To provide a spokesman for the Speaker and the majority party on the floor, the position of majority leader evolved (at first appointed by the Speaker and later elected by the majority conference). The Speaker relies on the majority leader to prepare the weekly schedule of business for the chamber, calling up bills to debate and vote.

In the era of industrialism that followed the Civil War, the House modernized its committee and floor procedures to deal with the increasingly complicated economic and social issues it faced. These issues prompted more orderly rules and division of labor within the committee system. As members began to stay in office longer and make careers out of their congressional service, seniority became the standard path to gaining influence and chairing committees. (Political scientists have called this development the "institutionalization" of Congress.)

In 1880 the House created a new standing committee on Rules, which became critical to the Speaker's power. Since then, whenever a controversial bill is called up, the Rules Committee will define the length of debate and the type of amendments that can be offered on the floor. This allows the Speaker and the majority leader to know essentially what the bill will consist of and when the vote will occur. Late nineteenth-century Speakers chaired the Rules Committee and used it to tame an unruly House. During the Progressive Era, Speaker Joseph G. Cannon (R-Illinois) single-handedly thwarted reform initiatives. The cigar-chomping "Uncle Joe" Cannon's dictatorial style eventually sparked rebellion by reformers, who in 1910 forced a vote to remove the Speaker from the Rules Committee. Chairmen of the Rules Committee then became independent powers who often strayed from their party's agenda. By 1961, when a coalition of conservative Democrats and Republicans ran the Rules Committee, liberals sought to reverse the earlier reforms. Speaker Sam Rayburn lent his immense personal prestige to an effort that expanded the membership of the Rules Committee and diluted the power of its chair. Speakers no longer chaired the committee, but they appointed the majority members, turning it into an agent of the leadership.

1. Joseph G. Cannon, the powerful Speaker of the House from 1903 to 1911.

In the 1970s, liberal reformers in the Democratic conference stripped the House Ways and Means Committee of its authority to appoint members to committees, shifting that power to the parties' steering committees, under the control of the party leaders. Speaker Jim Wright (D-Texas) further consolidated the power of the leadership, until he was brought down on ethics charges raised by Newt Gingrich (R-Georgia), leader of the conservative wing of the minority party. When Republicans returned to the majority in 1995, after forty years in the minority, Speaker Gingrich embraced and expanded Wright's lead in centralizing power under his own control. House Republicans set term limits for committee chairs and gave the Speaker authority to pass over the senior members of his party and pick more like-minded members as chairs.

Ninety years after Representative Jeannette Rankin (R-Montana) became the first woman to serve in Congress, Nancy Pelosi (D-California) "broke the marble ceiling" to become Speaker in 2007. Although the opposite of Gingrich ideologically, she continued his centralized tendencies. Speaker Pelosi became the face and voice of her party, frequently addressing issues on the House floor. She overruled committee chairs in bringing controversial legislation directly to the floor without their committees' approval. Senate majority leader Harry Reid (D-Nevada) observed with admiration: "She runs the House with an iron hand."

The House minority leadership operates at a disadvantage since the rules favor those who have the votes; the House majority can prevail without bothering to consult the minority. The minority leader focuses instead on positioning the minority to provoke the opposition and appeal to the voters. The job of the minority is largely to keep the majority honest, presenting legislative alternatives that have little chance of passing but that might attract media attention. The minority will try to force votes, despite their limited ability to offer amendments on the floor.

One tactic available to them has been a motion to recommit a bill to committee. Since a motion to recommit can be amended, the minority will use it as a vehicle for an amendment that appeals to public opinion, but which the majority party does not want to pass. Once the majority votes it down, the minority has a campaign issue.

Representatives take pride in calling themselves "the people's House," as that body is the only part of the federal government that has always been directly elected. No one can be appointed to the House. If a representative dies or resigns, the states hold special elections to fill vacancies (unlike Senate vacancies, where most governors can make short-term appointments). Every member of the House stands for election every two years and takes the oath of office anew at the beginning of the new Congress. By starting fresh, the majority can revise the House rules by a majority vote at the start of the Congress, and it can make significant changes in procedure, particularly if a new majority has just come to power, eager to reverse the way things were done.

The two-year election cycle (the shortest term of office among world legislatures) keeps House members perpetually running and raising funds. Reapportionment after each national census requires the states to redraw their congressional boundaries. The party that holds the majority in the state legislature invariably creates districts that favor its own candidates by sorting registered voters in a manner that guarantees "safe districts." They do this by "packing"—concentrating the opposition into one district—or "cracking"—distributing opponents into as many districts as possible to reduce their clout. The familiar term for these practices, "Gerrymandering," dates back to 1812, when Massachusetts Governor Elbridge Gerry's party in the state legislature concocted some odd-shaped congressional districts. An editorial cartoonist added a salamander's head and wings and gave it the governor's name. The term and the practice stuck. Combined with their overwhelming advantage in fund-raising and name recognition, modern House incumbents enjoy a 96 percent rate of reelection.

A failed constitutional amendment in 1791 would have pegged the population of every congressional district at fifty thousand. Had that been ratified, there would be some six thousand representatives in the House today. Instead, the average congressional district now contains about 690,000 inhabitants. Critics believe this population growth has lessened the type of constituent contact that once existed and have recommended expanding the House membership. The columnist George Will once asked: "Why not have 1,000 Congressmen?" But after assessing the reasons for change, he conceded that the "sheer cumbersomeness" of such a large body would likely preclude it.

## The cooling Senate

Whenever House members considered running for the Senate, Speaker Sam Rayburn would grumble: "Why would you do that? You're already in Washington." Rayburn had a point. Members of both bodies earn the same salaries, and representatives, though they run more frequently, have safer seats that almost guarantee reelection. But being a senator carries more prominence and individual authority. Because the Senate does so much of its work by unanimous consent, senators gain power as soon as they take office. Senators therefore attract more media attention, which can fuel presidential ambitions. (For all the senators who have run for president, only three have gone directly to the White House, the rest being "too loaded up with baggage and compromise" for what reporters have called the "message-driven simplicity" of a presidential campaign.)

Senators occupy historic desks in the chamber, carving their names inside the desk drawers alongside those of prominent predecessors. They vote by voice (which takes from fifteen to twenty minutes, about the same as the House takes to vote electronically). Senators have more opportunity to amend bills on the floor and to block objectionable actions. While the House rules favor an organized majority, the Senate's rules give more muscle to the minority.

In creating a bicameral system, James Madison saw the Senate as "a necessary fence." Selected by state legislatures, senators would serve six-year terms, and only one-third would stand in each congressional election. Madison trusted that this would insulate the Senate from shifting public opinion so it therefore could proceed "with more coolness, with more system, and with more wisdom, than the popular branch." Later in the nineteenth century, a story spread that may be apocryphal yet captured the Senate's essence. It claimed that when Thomas Jefferson returned from France after the Constitution had been adopted, he questioned George Washington on why the new government needed a Senate. Washington asked, "Why did you pour your coffee into your saucer?" "To cool it," Jefferson replied. "That is precisely why we created the Senate," said Washington, "to cool it."

Jefferson contributed to the Senate's distinct ethos during his vice presidency by preparing a manual of parliamentary practice (which the House also adopted). He believed that "order, decency, and regularity" would produce "a dignified public body." Political issues would invariably generate heat and emotion, but tensions could be defused through polite language. Senators should therefore not refer to each other by name ("the distinguished senior senator from the great state of…") and address the presiding officer rather than each other in debate (which is why they punctuate their remarks with "Mr. President" or "Madam President"). They should not insult each other, question each other's motives, or disparage each other's states. Anyone breaking these rules can be ordered to take their seat and stop participating further in the day's debate. Senior members will take junior colleagues aside to advise them on appropriate behavior in the chamber.

The snail's pace of legislative deliberations can frustrate the new senators, impatient to enact legislation and reform government practices. Senators who left business careers, or were governors, had been used to setting their own schedules. In the Senate they encounter endless discussion, debate, and delay. Former Governor Henry Bellmon (R-Oklahoma) regarded the Senate as a letdown. "Compared to the responsibility, work load, and excitement of the four years as governor," he concluded, "serving in the U.S. Senate seemed about as exciting as watching a stump rot."

The U.S. Senate has been called the most powerful "upper house" of any democratic government. In the First Congress, that label simply described its location upstairs over the larger House chamber in Federal Hall. Public attention focused far more on the House at first, while the Senate devoted itself largely to perfecting legislation passed by the other body. For six years the Senate met entirely in secret and, even after opening its doors, got much less press attention than the House. In 1806 Senator William Plumer (Federalist-New Hampshire) complained that few visitors sat in the Senate galleries, whereas the House galleries were always packed.

The Senate's evolution into a more commanding body began with a compromise designed to defuse the emotional issue of human slavery in the western territories. When alarm was raised over Missouri's admission into the Union as a slave-owning state, the Compromise of 1820 preserved the balance between the North and South by admitting Maine as a free state. The Compromise drew a line across the nation, prohibiting slavery north of that line and pairing the admission of new states from the two sections. That meant that on the most divisive issue of the day, the Senate would be evenly divided. As public attention shifted to the Senate, with it came such ambitious representatives as Henry Clay (Whig-Kentucky), Daniel Webster (Whig-Massachusetts), and John C. Calhoun (D-South Carolina), whose oratory created the Senate's Golden Age of Debate.

2. The "Great Compromiser," Henry Clay, served as Speaker of the House and as leader of his party in the Senate.

As the territories lined up to become states, the Senate and House outgrew their space. There had been 34 senators and 142 representatives in 1810, when they first occupied their elegant chambers on the Capitol's second floor, but there were 62 senators and 234 representatives by 1851, when Congress authorized construction of two wings on the Capitol to house enlarged chambers. In 1859, 66 senators marched from their old chamber to the new, in a procession that contained men who would serve in the cabinets and the military of both the Union and the Confederacy.

The post–Civil War industrial revolution saw an expansion of the American economy and the federal government. Senate committees dealing with tariffs, taxes, and appropriations grew independently powerful, and wealthy men competed for Senate seats to influence economic development. During the Progressive Era, muckraking journalists accused the Senate of acting more for special interests than for the public good. Charges surfaced that some state legislators had accepted bribes to vote for Senate candidates; and dissension in the state legislature allowed some Senate seats to remain vacant for an entire Congress. Rather than adopt the European model of trimming the power of the upper house, American progressives transferred the power to elect senators from the legislature to a direct vote by the people. Reformers hoped that this change would circumvent the corrupt political machines that often controlled the legislatures. The Seventeenth Amendment was ratified in 1913, and the next year the voters reelected every incumbent who was running. The state legislatures had not been far removed from public opinion.

Direct election turned out to be significant for what it did *not* change. The Seventeenth Amendment left all of the Senate's original powers intact. It made senators closer to the people of their states, whose votes they courted for reelection. A few critics have advocated its repeal on the grounds that it weakened the ties between the states and the federal government, but the voters are unlikely ever to relinquish the right to choose their U.S. senators.

With two-thirds of the senators continuing in office through each election, the Senate has defined itself as a "continuing body." It does not enact new rules by majority vote at the beginning of each new Congress the way that the House does, which makes changing Senate rules much more complicated and infrequent. "Administrations come and go," observed the scholarly Senator Henry Cabot Lodge (R-Massachusetts). "Houses assemble and disperse, Senators change, but the Senate is always there in the Capitol, and always organized, with an existence unbroken since 1789."

The Senate operates according to a small number of standing rules, which it regularly waives by unanimous consent agreements. Floyd Riddick, who served as Senate parliamentarian, insisted that the rules were perfect, "and if they change every one of them, the rules will be perfect." What he meant was that the Senate adopted rules to fit its needs and had the constitutional power to rewrite all of them if they no longer worked. Senate rules allow more time for debate and delay than in the House, which requires more negotiation and compromise to get anything done. The resulting slow pace frustrates nearly everyone, but shields against hastily enacting flawed bills.

While the House is ruled from the chair, the Senate is ruled from the floor, by its members rather than its presiding officer. Other than to break an occasional tie, the president of the Senate (the vice president of the United States) has only the authority that the Senate willingly grants. Vice presidents can make parliamentary rulings, but senators can overturn them by a simple majority vote. Vice presidents can address the Senate only with its indulgence. The first vice president, John Adams, interjected himself so often in the debate during the First Congress that his friends warned against stirring up controversy, and Adams quieted down. Vice presidents have served as liaisons between the administration and Congress, but Vice President Spiro Agnew once made the mistake of buttonholing a senator on the floor to solicit his vote.

Although he was from Agnew's party, the angry senator publicly announced that if the vice president did that again, he would vote the opposite way. Through a combination of imposed and self-imposed restraints, therefore, vice presidents have presided in a neutral manner and limited their appearances in the chamber mostly to ceremonial occasions.

In the vice president's absence, the Senate elects a president pro tempore, customarily the senior member of the majority party. Although the position stands third in the line of presidential succession, it has been held by senators in their eighties and nineties. The real leader of the Senate, the majority leader, is not mentioned in the Constitution because political parties did not exist when it was written. During the nineteenth century, the Senate operated without floor leaders, with the chair of the majority conference calling bills off the legislative calendar for debate. In 1913, President Woodrow Wilson persuaded Senate Democrats to designate a floor leader to manage his legislative agenda, and John Worth Kern (D-Indiana) became the first majority leader. Since 1937, both party floor leaders have claimed the front row center seats in the Senate chamber and have been afforded the right of first recognition. Whenever several senators are seeking permission to speak at the same time, the presiding officer will call on the majority and minority leaders first, giving them possession of the floor, which offers a significant parliamentary advantage.

Opponents of a bill may block it by holding the floor and conducting a filibuster. The term comes from the Dutch word for freebooter, or pirate, and has been applied to the minority of senators who seize control of the proceedings against the majority. If a vote were held, the majority would prevail, so the minority filibusters to stop a vote from occurring. The Hollywood movie *Mr. Smith Goes to Washington* fixed the public image of a filibuster as that of a single senator talking himself hoarse while holding the floor for hours. These days, filibusters often involve no talking at all, just someone applying the rules to tie the Senate into procedural knots, or a cloture motion that fails to get the sixty votes needed to cut off debate.

The Senate had no cloture rule at all until 1917, when a "little group of willful men," as President Wilson called them, filibustered against arming American merchant ships against German submarine warfare. The wartime atmosphere prompted the Senate to establish a cloture rule, by which a two-thirds vote could cut off debate. For the next half century, filibusters became the almost exclusive tool of southern senators intent on blocking civil rights legislation. Cloture was rarely invoked until one ended a fifty-seven-day filibuster against the Civil Rights Act of 1964. In 1975, Senate liberals reduced the cloture requirement from two-thirds (sixty-seven votes) to three-fifths (sixty votes). Since parties rarely enjoy majorities of sixty votes, a straight party-line vote is therefore insufficient to pass controversial legislation.

Views on the filibuster depend on whether one's party is in the majority or the minority. The majority denounces obstructionism, while the minority defends such tactics as a defense against being steamrollered. Frustrated with filibusters against judicial nominations, Senate Majority Leader Bill Frist (R-Tennessee) threatened a "nuclear option" by which the presiding officer could rule the debate dilatory and force a vote. If the minority protested, a majority vote of the Senate could sustain the ruling of the chair. This would effectively reduce cloture to a simple majority vote. It took its name "nuclear" because of the devastation it could wreak on Senate traditions. Opponents claimed that the nuclear option would end robust debate, making the Senate another version of the House, and a bipartisan group of veteran senators worked out a compromise that averted the nuclear option.

With rules that foster deliberation, cooperation, and consensus building, the majority cannot relegate the minority to the role of bystanders. The majority leader sets the agenda by calling bills from the calendar, but the minority leader holds an arsenal of parliamentary weapons for blocking action. Little of consequence happens in the Senate, therefore, unless the two party leaders have reached some accord. Even then, dissenters from either party can derail their efforts. The Senate's procedures make it "the negotiating body." Having passed a strong bill, House members get infuriated over compromises struck in the Senate. But the House minority will often give thanks for the Senate minority's ability to force changes or derail a bill entirely. Senate leaders regularly remind their House counterparts that their chambers operate differently and that the Senate majority cannot do everything it wants. Senator Arlen Specter (R/D-Pennsylvania) has compared the Senate's rules to anarchy and the House rules to despotism, adding that deciding which is better "is a fairly tough choice."

## To get along, go along

"Young man, I want you to remember, you can't have everything your own way," the Speaker of the House told Carl Hayden (D-Arizona) when he was first elected in 1912. "There never was an important piece of legislation enacted by Congress which was not the result of compromise." Hayden was fond of repeating that quote to freshmen until he left Congress in 1969. Those words were echoed by a later Speaker, Sam Rayburn, who advised new members: "If you want to get along, go along."

The legislative process is one of continuous bargaining. Strong individuals win election to Congress, where they will need to work collectively in order to accomplish anything. They must tailor their ideas to gain majority support, often merging their objectives into larger packages filled with other provisions. They must build coalitions, drum up publicity, plan parliamentary strategy, debate, and haggle to garner enough votes to get the bill passed. That is just to clear one house. The process must start again in the other house. Then the two versions must be reconciled before going to the president.

Compromise, negotiation, and bipartisanship have also been crucial for foreign policy. President Woodrow Wilson proved unable to convince the Senate to approve the Treaty of Versailles, which ended World War I and established the League of Nations, partly because he had not included senators in the negotiations. After World War II, Democratic President Harry Truman relied heavily on Senator Arthur Vandenberg (R-Michigan) to promote a bipartisan foreign policy. Having shifted his own thinking from isolationist to internationalist, Vandenberg worked to unite both parties behind Truman's Cold War programs. To win Senate approval for the Marshall Plan for rebuilding postwar Europe, Vandenberg advised the Truman administration not to request the entire $17 billion for a four-year program, but only the appropriations needed for the first year of the program, giving opponents a smaller target. He appreciated that legislation was "the art of the possible," and that, no matter what their inherent qualities, bills had to be made politically palatable.

Sometimes called the Senate's "odd couple," Edward (Ted) Kennedy (D-Massachusetts) and Orrin Hatch (R-Utah) successfully cosponsored some notable health legislation despite being poles apart ideologically. Hatch attributed this to Kennedy's willingness "to work with those who shared his goals, even if they had different ideas on how to achieve them." There remains the danger, however, that too much compromise can dilute worthwhile ideas and produce less effective legislation. Some members are unwilling to compromise their principles in order to achieve influence. One longtime Senate staffer, Howard Shuman, observed that the durability of congressional reputations depended on whether a member's passion was for power or for issues. The ability to make one's colleagues tremble was no guarantee against being forgotten. Instead, it was the issue-oriented member who stood for something, who survived the test of time.

A notable example of standing against party and public opinion occurred in 1950 when Margaret Chase Smith (R-Maine) issued her "Declaration of Conscience" against the "fear, ignorance, bigotry, and smear" being employed by such congressional anti-Communist investigators as Joseph R. McCarthy (R-Wisconsin). Another courageous stand occurred in 1995, when Mark Hatfield (R-Oregon), chairman of the Senate Appropriations Committee, cast the vote that cost his party the two-thirds margin they needed to approve a Balanced Budget Amendment to the Constitution. Having concluded that the convoluted amendment would cause more problems than it would solve, Hatfield voted no, although it jeopardized his chairmanship. Congress afterward managed to balance the budget without the amendment.

As James Madison wrote in *The Federalist*, society is composed of a "great variety of interests, parties and sects," and the difficulty in creating coalitions to form a majority reduces the danger of the majority trampling the rights of the minority. Congress reflects Madison's vision of pluralism made of contending self-interests. Members who forge compromises to pass bills implore their colleagues not to "let the perfect be the enemy of the good." A sponsor of a major farm bill, passed over the president's veto in 2008, conceded that it was not a perfect bill and that it contained some provisions he wished were not there. "But it is a massive piece of legislation, as is every farm bill," he explained, "and we have to reach compromise to be able to get a bill of that massive size passed by the House and by the Senate." Critics could decry the legislation as "pork-barrel politics" or as localism driving national policy, but its authors had crafted a package that addressed the needs of producers and consumers as broadly as possible in every region. That is the essence of representative government.

# Chapter 2
# **Campaigns and constituents**

Faced with staggering federal deficits when he came to office in 1993, President Bill Clinton proposed an economic plan that combined spending cuts with a tax increase that fell hardest on wealthier taxpayers. House Republicans voted unanimously against the tax increase, joined by enough fiscally conservative Democrats to tie the tally at 217–217. That left the freshman Marjorie Margolies-Mezvinsky (D-Pennsylvania) to cast the deciding vote. Calls from her constituents were running overwhelmingly against the plan, making it clear how much the affluent suburbs of Philadelphia she represented disliked bearing the brunt of the taxes. Margolies-Mezvinsky had already announced her opposition to the plan, on the grounds that the spending cuts did not go deeply enough, but in the Democratic cloakroom off the House floor she took a call from Clinton, who pleaded that the fate of his presidency hinged on her vote. When she reluctantly voted "yes," she heard other representatives calling out "Bye-bye, Marjorie." Although the economic plan succeeded, Margolies-Mezvinsky lost her race for reelection. Reviewing her single term, she felt that the question she had to answer was: "Do you represent, or do you lead? In the end, one must put aside all the chatter, noise, all the headlines, all the calls, close the door to your office, and make a very tough and often unpopular choice."

Elected locally, candidates for Congress go to Washington to craft national policy, and they find that voting on major legislation may force them to choose between national needs and constituent approval. They must calculate the impact of their votes on their chances of reelection. They return home regularly to monitor local sentiments, which in turn will influence how they vote on legislation. They also want to point out the federal projects they have brought home, on the assumption that constituents will ask: "What have you done for me lately?" Representative L. Mendel Rivers (D-South Carolina) was a classic case; he won reelection for thirty years on the strength of his seniority on the Armed Services Committee (which ensured that every branch of the military operated a base in his district) under the unambiguous campaign slogan "Rivers Delivers."

Elections give the voters a chance to make their own opinions known. They can decree continuity or change, demand a more active or limited government, tilt toward an ideology, or simply endorse a candidate's individual qualities. Voters reelect incumbents to allow them to gain seniority and clout in Congress, or turn out in reaction against the drift of national policy. It is an oddity that while opinion polls rank Congress poorly as a whole, voters are most likely to reelect their own senators and representatives. Citizens like the way their own members are representing them; they just dislike everyone else's. Feeding this perception, candidates will often run for Congress by running against it, using the institution's collective unpopularity as a campaign tool, differentiating themselves, as one member explained to a political scientist, from "the rest of those bandits down there in Congress."

## Campaigning for Congress

"I am going to Texas, and you can go to hell," Representative Davy Crockett (Whig-Tennessee) told off his constituents when they failed to reelect him in 1834—two years before he died at the Alamo. Since federal elections began in 1788, candidates for Congress have campaigned vigorously by horseback, wagon, railroad, plane, car, and bus. Nineteenth-century candidates became accomplished stump speakers, able to address huge crowds without amplification. On his deathbed, former senator and vice president John C. Breckinridge (D-Kentucky) impressed his doctor with his clear and strong voice. "Why doctor," the old politician said proudly, "I can throw my voice a mile." His successors could address the voters via radio, television, and the Internet. In the 1920s, candidates had to adjust to the unseen audiences of radio. The new medium fit their florid stump style of speaking, although some tied themselves to the microphone to keep from pacing the stage by habit. In the 1950s, politicians fixed on television as the best means of reaching statewide audiences. The cooler medium required a different style of presentation and influenced the type of candidates who got elected.

Politicians rank personal contact highly but recognize that the kind of face-to-face campaigning they can do will not reach many people statewide or in districts with hundreds of thousands of constituents. They jockey to appear on camera and devote the largest share of their campaign spending to television ads. As early as the 1930s, the humorist Will Rogers commented that politics had gotten so expensive that "it takes a lot of money even to get beat with." Raising campaign funds consumes an inordinate amount of each member's time and has contributed to truncating the congressional workweek to Tuesday through Thursday. Since fund-raising also provides access for lobbyists, it has become a political issue. Campaign financing reforms now require congressional candidates to disclose how much they raise and spend, and the names of their contributors. But in *Buckley v. Valeo* (1976), the Supreme Court struck down legislation aimed at capping the cost of campaigns. The justices decreed that candidates could not be limited in the amount of their own money they spent on their own campaigns. Opponents called such caps a

3. **Campaigning can be joyous as well as arduous. Here Senate minority leader Everett M. Dirksen (R-Illinois) and Charles Mathias (R-Maryland) christen a campaign bus at the Capitol in 1968.**

restriction on free speech, while proponents argued that unlimited individual spending favored the independently wealthy. Money talks, and those with more can talk more loudly.

Despite various reform efforts, the cost of campaigning has continued to escalate. Congressional candidates have grown dependent on a proliferating number of Political Action Committees (PACs) to serve as their fund-raisers. Sponsored by special-interest and single-issue groups, as well as by aspiring leaders in Congress, PACs spread funds to multiple candidates to win support for their causes. After an election, PACs will often help the winners retire their campaign debts and prepare for the next race. Money raised for a specific candidate is known as "hard money," whereas money raised for general get-out-the-vote campaigns and not tied to a specific candidate is called "soft money" and is less closely regulated than hard money. In seeking soft money, the national party organizations offered large donors opportunities to meet privately with the most influential committee chairmen. National associations in turn hosted fund-raisers for the committee chairs handling legislation that they wanted to see passed. The McCain-Feingold Act of 2002 attempted to ban "soft money," but opponents have been creative in seeking ways to circumvent it.

Once in office, the time between elections speeds past. Since the term of every member of the House, from the Speaker down to the freshman class, will expire in two years, representatives run constantly until they lose, retire, or die. In their districts, House members relentlessly seek out constituents in storefronts and at state fairs and community meetings. Representative Gene Snyder (R-Kentucky) made it a routine to drive the length of Highway 42, which ran through his district, stopping randomly at coffee shops and barbershops to find out what was on people's minds. Even with their longer terms, senators follow similar routines. Although politicians rely heavily on pollsters for monitoring public opinion, members of Congress often find that regular traveling around their states precludes the need for expensive polls, since they can talk to more people in a weekend than the pollsters will cover. Senator Richard Russell (D-Georgia) used to say that the six-year term permitted senators to spend two years as a statesman, two years as a politician, and two years as a demagogue. But members of the House cannot afford "the luxury of being a statesman, as a senator can," commented Representative Fletcher Thompson (R-Georgia). "A congressman runs every two years. He can't run very far from basic public opinion in his district or he won't get reelected."

Incumbents say that there are only two ways to run for reelection: scared, or unopposed. Even faced with opposition, representatives enjoy a high rate of reelection, partly because of the greater name recognition that comes with holding office and partly because their parties in the state legislature drew the congressional boundaries to maximize the party's strength in the district. Most districts are solidly Democratic or Republican. Some marginal districts will swing back and forth, particularly during presidential election years. Safe seats sometimes encourage members to keep a low profile in Washington. They will rarely cosponsor amendments or speak on the floor, and will devote themselves to promoting the needs of their district and responding to constituent requests. Regular reelection will allow them to rise quietly through the ranks to influence policy.

Safe seats can disappear, however. Districts may be merged, after a census, forcing colleagues to run against each other in a primary to claim the new district. Despite its 96 percent rate of reelection, House membership is never stagnant. Deaths, retirements, runs for other offices, and defeats produce an average turnover in House membership that will range from 10 to 20 percent after each election. At any given time, half of the members of the House will have served for fewer than eleven years.

## Political parties in Congress

The Constitution does not mention political parties, because some of the framers prayed that divisive "factions" might be avoided. But parties promptly developed in the early republic and became an essential force in congressional policy making. The center aisle in the House and Senate chambers divide the two major parties. Each has its own cloakroom, elects its own leaders, and holds its own conferences. The political parties select their own members' committee assignments. The party leaders and the committee chairs and ranking minority party members manage legislative business in the chambers. The majority party plans and drives the legislative agenda with the minority taking every opportunity to reshape it. Legislation inevitably reflects the tension between the parties, in committee and on the floor, adding a political element to the checks and balances between the branches.

The first signs of political parties emerged as early as the ratification of the Constitution in 1788, when its supporters and opponents roughly divided into Federalists and Anti-Federalists. Federalists controlled the first three Congresses until 1795, when the opposition (by then becoming known as Democratic-Republicans) gained the majority in the House. In the elections of 1800, Federalists lost both houses, never to regain power. After several decades of one-party rule, known as the "Era of Good Feelings," Congress in the 1830s divided politically between President Andrew Jackson's supporters, the Democrats, and his opponents, the Whigs. Both parties combined northern and southern wings. The explosive issue of slavery in the territories would eventually undermine the Whig Party, whose northern members merged with anti-slavery Democrats and other factions to become Republicans. Since 1857, the Republican and Democratic parties have dominated Congress.

Given the size and diversity of the United States, the persistence of a two-party system in Congress has been extraordinary. Among the contributing factors is the constitutional requirement of electing presidents through the Electoral College. The parties' need to put together a majority of electors from across the nation has encouraged them to be broad-based and inclusive, discouraging ideologically focused third parties or regionally based parties. The Texas billionaire Ross Perot, for example, largely self-funded his 1992 campaign and received 19.7 million popular votes, but he did not win a single electoral vote, causing his Reform Party to fade away. The two-party system has been reinforced in Congress by the states' practice of electing representatives by district rather than statewide (districts are not required by the Constitution). Occasionally, third parties have held congressional seats, but their presence has been fleeting. Independents who are elected to Congress need to join one of the major party caucuses in order to get decent committee assignments. "You don't have to be a political genius to know that if you function alone, there are real limits to what you can accomplish," commented Bernie Sanders (I-Vermont), an Independent who caucused with the Democrats in both houses.

Beneath the big tents of the two-party system, however, lurk conflicting ideologies that have often been apparent within the parties' congressional conferences. Since the Civil War, the Democrats had been an amalgamation of rural southern whites and northern urban immigrants. Republicans remained strongest in New England and the Midwest, and various reform movements occasionally elected members to Congress from the West. Throughout the twentieth century, Congress therefore operated under a de facto four-party system, with a coalition of conservative Democrats and Republican voting against liberals in both parties. In 1912, Theodore Roosevelt split the Republican Party by running for president as a Progressive. The Republican Party remained divided for decades between eastern liberals and midwestern conservatives. At the same time, conservative southerners constituted a significant minority within the Democratic Party, accruing seniority that gave them most of the major committee chairmanships. Passage of the Civil Rights Act of 1964 saw the breakup of the "Solid South," profoundly changing patterns of congressional elections. For a century, the Congressional map had followed the old Missouri Compromise line, with Democrats largely representing districts below and Republicans above the line (except in the larger cities), neatly bisecting the nation from East to West. By the end of the twentieth century, the Congressional map instead resembled a Jackson Pollock painting. As all of the regions became more politically competitive, the Republican and Democratic conferences in the House and Senate grew more internally cohesive, with fewer middle-of-the-road members willing to cross the line for the sake of bipartisanship. Straight party-line votes in Congress, so rare in the past when the parties were internally divided, now became commonplace.

Every four years, a candidate for Congress will run on the same ticket as the party's presidential nominee. Should they both win, the popularity of the presidential candidate in the district or state will often influence their relationship in office. If the presidential nominee happens to be unpopular in a state or district, the congressional candidate will run a local campaign that steers clear of the national ticket, and he or she will be nowhere to be seen when the presidential candidate makes a local appearance. If a congressional candidate wins election by a larger margin than the president, the White House will find it difficult to convince the member to vote for bills that are unpopular back home. If a successful candidate believes victory was due to the president's coattails, the member will support the president out of gratitude and self-preservation. Unpopular presidents can wreak havoc on their parties in Congress. Jimmy Carter came to the presidency in 1977 with Democrats holding large majorities in the House and Senate, but he alienated those who should have been his supporters and consequently suffered a number of legislative setbacks. When Carter lost in 1980, his early-evening concession depressed voter-turnout in the West, where the polls remained open for several more hours, costing some prominent Democrats their seats and the majority in the Senate. The collapse of Bill Clinton's ambitious health care plan in 1994 contributed to his party's loss of its majorities in both the Senate and House during the congressional midterm elections. Republicans dominated Congress from then until the midterm elections in 2006, when George W. Bush's war in Iraq and mishandling of Hurricane Katrina relief enabled Democrats to regain the majority.

Prior to the advent of the primary system for nominating congressional candidates, party bosses routinely selected candidates who had worked their way up through the ranks. Progressive reformers promoted primary elections, to let the people decide, and these often resulted in the election of candidates who were independent entrepreneurs, who could self-finance their campaigns, and who would be less responsive to party discipline. The congressional parties have also done their

best to influence the results. In both the House and Senate, the party conferences appoint congressional campaign committees to recruit candidates, provide resources for public opinion polling, raise funds, and advise how to spend them. House majority leader Tom DeLay (R-Texas) compared the national campaign committees to clubs that exist principally for their members. "The main benefit of membership is the gobs and gobs of campaign cash, or at least access to it, for others who are at risk, and who find themselves in a competitive election," DeLay observed. "But it's a two-way street. In order to have this collective political insurance, you have to pay a premium: You're expected to contribute a certain amount of money to the club, a negotiable amount based on your seniority, reelection security, committee assignments, etc. And if needed, you must be willing to travel and work on behalf of other at-risk members."

When the votes are counted, the loser may challenge the results. The Constitution leaves it to each house of Congress to determine whether a candidate should be seated. A disputed victor might be seated "without prejudice" while a committee investigates the charges. Two contested elections are instructive of the different ways the two houses of Congress operate. After the 1974 elections, the Senate Rules Committee spent months trying to recount the paper ballots from New Hampshire, where both candidates claimed victory. When they could not agree on who actually won, the senators sent the election back to the state, where in September 1975 the Democrat won the seat in a new election. By contrast, in the 1984 election an incumbent, Frank McCloskey (D-Indiana), initially won by seventy-two votes. After a recount, his Republican challenger Richard McIntyre went ahead by thirty-four. Indiana certified McIntyre the victor. Then the Democratic majority in the House held its own recount and declared that McCloskey won by four votes. House Republicans tried to declare the seat vacant and force a new election, but Democrats voted to seat McCloskey. The federal courts allowed this selection to stand, but the outraged Republican minority used the contested election as a rallying cry, and partisanship in the House grew more intense.

Only rarely has Congress refused to seat a member. In 1865, northerners in Congress barred all the members elected from the former Confederacy until those states ratified the Thirteenth Amendment, abolishing slavery. The House and Senate also excluded a few members for reasons ranging from questions of citizenship to malfeasance, disloyalty, and religious affiliation. In 1919, the House did not seat Victor Burger, a Wisconsin Socialist who had been convicted of violating the Espionage Act of 1917 for publishing articles against American participation in World War I. After the Supreme Court overturned his conviction, however, Berger served three terms in the House. In 1967 the House excluded Adam Clayton Powell (D-New York) out of disapproval of his freewheeling lifestyle. The Supreme Court reversed this action in 1969, on the grounds that Powell met all the constitutional requirements for service and had to be seated, although the House retained the constitutional authority to expel him by a two-thirds vote.

The states cannot set term limits on members of Congress, nor recall them by petition and state balloting. Some people assume that because their state constitution permits such practices for state officials that the same rules apply to senators and representatives. But no member of Congress has ever been recalled, nor ever will be until a constitutional amendment permits it. The courts have determined that the only qualifications for members are those specifically designated in the Constitution: age, citizenship, and residence.

## The freshman class

Fresh from victory, those elected for the first time arrive in Congress full of new ideas to enact, often impatient with the glacial pace of legislation. It takes a while to realize that the separation of powers means that their chamber is just part of the government, not the whole. A bill that sails through the House may go nowhere in the Senate. Legislators must package their ideas in such a way not only to convince their leadership, but also the other body, the president, and the courts. After a pivotal election, a new or expanded majority can trigger an initial burst of legislative activity, but over time the system of checks and balances works against rapid change. Freshman members also complain about the demands of the job, the inability to set their own schedules, the need to spend so much time away from their families, and the pressures of doing so much fund-raising, but they all run for reelection.

In their efforts to reform the system, a few freshman members have been so determined to cut federal spending and abolish pork-barrel politics that they vote against federal funds for their own districts. (The "pork barrel" expression dates back to antebellum plantation days, when field hands dipped into a large barrel of salt pork for their food; similarly, when legislators win federal funding for special projects in their districts, they are "bringing home the bacon.") Among the voters, this may not be a popular position. Members who survive close races are said to return to Congress "Housebroken," more willing to compromise in order to accommodate their constituents' demands. Those who study voting patterns in Congress observe that the longer that members stay in Congress the more they tend to "regress toward the means," moderating their ideological views to increase their chances of reelection.

Confronting the ever-present tension between national and local interests, the British political theorist and member of Parliament Edmund Burke told his constituents in 1774 that legislators must voice the "general reason of the whole" rather than "local prejudices." Burke asserted that a member must dare to "resist the desires of his constituents when his judgment assured him they were wrong." When he voted against his district's interests, however, those noble sentiments got Burke defeated for reelection in 1780.

National needs, party unity, and presidential pressure often force members to cast difficult votes. One senior representative, William Natcher (D-Kentucky), used to advise freshmen to "do what's right, then go home and explain to your people why you did it.... Some votes will take the skin off your back. If you explain, your people back home will put it back on." In studying representation, political scientists have divided members of Congress into delegates (who follow constituents' wishes) and trustees (who follow their own principles), recognizing that most will blend those impulses depending on the issue. The more directly something affects the voters, particularly economic policy, the more they expect their member to act as a servant of the constituency. Voters will usually show greater tolerance of a member's independent stance on more indirect issues, such as national defense and foreign policy.

In the House, members of the minority find it easier to break ranks and "vote their district" on issues where their party is going to lose anyhow. In the Senate, the minority leader needs to hold at least forty-one votes to prevent cloture and will remind the conference that their strength lies in standing together. The parties will also look for ways to let vulnerable freshmen score legislative victories that will enhance their prospects for reelection. A Louisiana representative who won an upset victory in a special election in 2008 was not appointed to either the Energy or Intelligence committee, but his party leaders allowed him to introduce the National Energy Security Intelligence Act, which passed by a vote of 414–0. But this accomplishment proved insufficient for him to win another term.

Each freshman class has become progressively more inclusive with regard to race, ethnicity, and gender. The growing ranks of the Congressional Women's Caucus have given women members more clout for promoting issues of significance to women, particularly in matters of health, education, and equality in the workplace. The Congressional Black Caucus similarly has promoted civil rights and economic opportunity. Begun as small contingents in Congress, they expanded in size and influence, with some of their members rising to chair important committees. Women and minority members of Congress enable the legislative branch to better represent the nation, but they still fall short of their actual proportions of the population. This has posed a conundrum for the state legislatures in drawing congressional boundaries. A "color-blind" decision that ignores race as a factor risks dividing minority constituents among several districts, reducing the chance of a minority member winning election. But drawing districts that concentrate racial or ethnic groups to ensure their election has been seen by the Supreme Court as a form of "political apartheid" that violates the Fourteenth Amendment's pledge of equal protection under the laws. The under-representation of minorities in Congress can also be attributed to the states that drew the districts, the parties that put up the candidates, the voters who cast the ballots, and the potential candidates who did not run.

## Serving constituents

In 1934, Kansas City's political boss Tom Pendergast advised newly elected Senator Harry Truman (D-Missouri) to "work hard, keep your mouth shut, and answer your mail." The basic duties of senators and representatives are legislation, education, and advocacy. Their legislative function includes holding hearings and reporting out bills, while education requires informing their constituents about the issues and explaining the stands they have taken. Advocacy involves pleading their constituents' interests and attitudes on national issues and providing them with constituent services.

Candidates to Congress may get elected by accident, House Speaker John McCormack (D-Massachusetts) once observed, but are "seldom reelected by accident." Reelection depends on keeping constituents convinced that they are best representing their interests. Responding to constituent requests can be as helpful for keeping a member in office as any legislative accomplishment, so casework occupies the bulk of the staff time of every congressional office. Members' offices are deluged with postal mail, email, and phone calls, expressing constituents' views, and the offices will solicit more by sending out questionnaires and holding town hall meetings. The awareness that constituents keep them in office fosters a customers-come-first attitude. Even the internationally minded J. William Fulbright (D-Arkansas), the erudite chairman of the Senate Foreign Relations Committee, once interrupted a debate in Geneva over nuclear weapons for NATO to protest European restrictions on importing U.S. chickens. Protecting Arkansas' chicken producers kept Fulbright in the Senate.

Americans have a First Amendment right to petition their government, and Congress has collected mountains of such petitions, from long scrolls to stacks of identically worded postcards that support or oppose an issue, or seek assistance. Until World War II, half of the legislative output consisted of private bills, designed to help a specific individual or group, whether to repay damages done to private property in wartime, to provide a pension, or to unite family members through immigration. Later, Congress dealt with these issues generally in larger bills, and the number of private bills dwindled. Most constituent services now involve straightening out a problem with Social Security or veterans' payments, getting a son or daughter into one of the military service academies, expediting a passport, or some other congressional intervention with the bureaucracy. Members confront major national issues, but they also take pride in the individual cases in which they made a difference in someone's life.

Before the Internet, a good share of congressional correspondence came via telegraph. One staffer recalled how the member he worked for handed him a stack of telegrams on a particular issue and told him to sort them into "for" and "against" piles. Without bothering to read them, the member voted for the bill because the "for" pile was higher. But another member who received ten thousand messages opposed to a bill that he supported dismissed them on the grounds that a lot more people than that had elected him.

Email began arriving in the 1990s, and within a decade it accounted for 80 percent of all congressional correspondence. Email has facilitated members' communication with their constituents, particularly after postal mail had to be delayed for irradiation following an anthrax incident in 2001. Advocacy groups and associations have found it easy to encourage groups to use the Internet to contact legislators. Grassroots organizations, such as labor unions, environmentalists, and pro- and anti-abortion rights groups, influence members of both parties. The flood of email can make it difficult for members to respond, and tardy or unanswered messages can raise ire among Internet users who expect instant gratification. Polls indicate that a majority of Americans do not believe their members of Congress, despite their efforts, were interested in what they had to say, which accounted for angry outbursts at some town hall meetings.

As quickly as a new technology develops, members will adopt it, especially younger members and those in the minority. Senators and representatives use Web surveys and have turned their Web sites into electronic newsletters. They participate in town meetings on the Internet, inviting home-state residents to participate in a telephone conference call with the lawmaker. A typical call will draw many times the number who would attend an actual town meeting in the district. In response, when a hot issue is being debated and a critical vote is pending, the "folks back home" will swamp the members' email and jam their phone lines with calls. Members are aware that those who feel passionately about an issue are the one most likely to write or call and that they will not hear from the vast majority of their constituents. But those who feel passionately are also the ones most motivated to vote, especially in primary elections.

Pages of almost every issue of the *Congressional Record* are filled with members' recognition of their constituents' accomplishments and significant milestones. They congratulate Eagle Scouts, celebrate golden anniversaries, and eulogize the recently departed. On the same day, for instance, the *Congressional Record* carried resolutions establishing a National Dysphagia Awareness Month and a National Corvette Day, and one honoring the life of the winemaker Robert Mondavi. One tradition that has now disappeared was the nineteenth-century practice of sending packages of seeds to rural constituents: at each session of Congress, every member received crates of vegetable, flower, and grass seed packets from the Agriculture Department, to reap good will back home.

Despite modern improvements in communications, members want to spend as much time as possible at home. Increasingly, they leave their families back home and visit on weekends, when they also schedule town meetings, address civic organizations, visit churches and synagogues, and drop into the local barber shops to listen to people's opinions and complaints. Members maintain district offices and station part of their staff there. In Washington, they host visiting constituents, run breakfast meetings, give tours, pose for photographs with students on class trips, and do anything else they can to remind the voters that they are working for them.

Patronage constitutes a more specialized form of constituent service. Members enjoy the opportunity to nominate people from their home states for appointments to the military academies. They make recommendations for U.S. attorneys and federal judges from their states and for any number of executive-branch appointments. A classic case in the nineteenth century involved Representative James Buffinton (R-Massachusetts), who hated to turn down a constituent seeking federal office. He developed a practice of giving everyone who asked a letter of recommendation to the executive departments. Government hiring clerks knew his system. When he signed his name Buffington, adding a "g," it indicated that he wanted the man appointed. When he wrote

it accurately as Buffinton, without the "g," he did not mean the endorsement to be taken seriously.

## Media relations and news coverage

Although members of Congress would prefer to talk directly to their constituents and not have their words filtered through journalists, they depend on the news media for electoral survival. Junior and minority members, who have little control over the schedule or the agenda, especially regard communication as an essential tool for getting their ideas across to the public, their colleagues, and the administration.

The popularly elected House threw its doors open to the press on its first day of operation in 1789, but senators, at the time elected by state legislatures, had no gallery and met in secret until 1795. Neither the Continental Congress nor the Constitutional Convention was conducted in public, and nothing in the Constitution requires Congress to legislate in public, only to publish a journal of its proceedings. In 1841 the Senate set aside a row of seats above its presiding officer, reserving them as the first press gallery—sixty years before the White House designated a press room. Congress has remained the most open branch of the federal government. Members love to talk and serve as ready sources of information for the media. Yet because Congress speaks in many voices, it is usually at a disadvantage when dealing with the president, who can dominate the news.

A bronze plaque in the Capitol commemorates the inventor Samuel F. B. Morse's first demonstration of the telegraph there in 1844. A congressional appropriation enabled Morse to run wires from Washington to Baltimore. "What hath God wrought" was the first message he sent from Washington. "What is the news from Washington" Baltimore responded (telegraph messages contained no punctuation). The telegraph became a mainstay of congressional communication from then until 1990, when the last machines were removed, finally rendered obsolete by new electronic communications. Whatever the communications technology available, Congress has seized on it avidly. Television coverage of hearings made national stars out of some legislators, beginning with Senator Estes Kefauver (D-Tennessee), whose investigation into organized crime drew national audiences in 1951 and propelled him into a presidential race. The cameras built up and then demolished the reputation of Wisconsin Senator Joseph R. McCarthy. His anti-Communist investigations gave him abundant TV time, until the televised Army-McCarthy hearings in 1954 exposed his bullying tactics and led to his censure by the Senate. Washington-based Sunday morning news programs such as *Face the Nation* and *Meet the Press* regularly give air time to members of Congress, who relish the opportunity to address the nation and influence fellow congressional members who tune in. Senator John F. Kennedy (D-Massachusetts) stood among the first in Congress to predict that the new media would play a decisive role in presidential elections.

Not until 1979 did the House permit the televising of its debates, a service provided by C-SPAN (Cable-Satellite Public Affairs Network). House members attracted so much national attention that the Senate relented in 1986 and let the cameras into its chamber. The bright lights changed the ambiance of the chambers and encouraged members to address their remarks to the cameras. TV cameras also became regular fixtures at committee hearings, news briefings, and other congressional events. It became a truism that the most dangerous place to stand in the Capitol was between a member of Congress and a television camera. By the 1990s, the Internet added a new layer of digital electronic communication, encouraging every senator and representative to maintain a Web site.

More than five thousand journalists representing every form of news media, from news organizations across the nation and around the world, hold press credentials for the congressional press galleries, although only a few dozen of them use the Capitol

**4. Press conferences are part of daily life at the Capitol.**

press galleries on a daily basis. Despite Congress's courting of the press corps, its relationship with the media has been punctuated by members complaining of bias and misrepresentation, and by reporters protesting against politicians attempting to manipulate the news. No matter how much members may complain about news reporting, however, they recognize that media provides their best link to the general public. News coverage will affect their chances of passing legislation, of returning for another term, and of climbing to higher office. This awareness has made Congress the most accessible branch of government to reporters. "They think the good opinion of the press is important to their reelections, which dominates much of their thinking," the veteran Washington correspondent James Reston explained why Congress operated so much in the open; "consequently they see reporters and some of them even read us."

# Chapter 3
# **In committee**

Having won election to the House or Senate, new members immediately scramble for their committee assignments. Committees will shape their legislative careers, helping them create a record, attract media attention, and raise campaign funds. As soon as Nancy Pelosi came to the House in 1987, she campaigned for a seat on the Appropriations Committee, pressing her case with the Democratic leadership. The coveted seat eluded her until after she won reelection. Members sometimes grow attached to unwanted assignments. Lee Hamilton (D-Indiana) asked to be on the House Public Works Committee, but to his disappointment wound up on Foreign Affairs. Before long, Hamilton developed such a strong interest in foreign policy that he turned down a seat on the powerful Ways and Means Committee and went on to chair Foreign Affairs.

When Woodrow Wilson wrote his doctoral dissertation on *Congressional Government* in 1885, he memorably described Congress in session as Congress on public exhibition, whereas Congress in its committee rooms was Congress at work. Legislation is crafted more in committee than on the floor of either chamber. A seat on a committee therefore gives a member a greater chance of influencing legislation on that issue than those outside the committee. Members devote much of their attention to committee work, grilling witnesses and marking up (revising) bills.

Senators and representatives serve on multiple committees and subcommittees, which might meet simultaneously, forcing them to choose among them or to come and go between them (and rely more on committee staff). The legislative day divides members' attention between committees and floor actions. They might be hearing testimony on an urgent national matter when bells summon them to the chamber for a vote, forcing prominent witnesses to cool their heels in the interim. But no matter how chaotic and exhausting the schedules, committees remain the heart of the legislative process.

At the opening of a new Congress, the parties' steering committees give the new members their committee assignments, and some of the senior members shift to fill vacancies on more desirable committees. The number of seats on a committee available to each party is generally proportional to the party margins in the full chamber. Party conferences also set limits on the number of committees on which members can serve. Committees receive varying levels of operating funds to hire their own staff, with the majority party controlling the resources and sharing a portion with the minority.

The rules of the House and Senate define the jurisdiction of each committee, dividing the major issues of government between them. Committees are subdivided into subcommittees for further specialization, and they shoulder most of the work. Subcommittees cull through the many bills introduced, eliminate most, and focus on a few. Their staffs gather information to be used in hearings, which will call expert witnesses, attract media attention, and build a case for passing the legislation. Subcommittees then report to the full committee, which may hold its own hearings. The hearings of some of the "prestige committees" regularly make news, while others are more policy oriented and attract less public attention—their members having to be content with making legislation rather than headlines. Veterans advise newcomers to be workhorses rather than show horses, but ambitious freshmen still come to Congress with visions of serving on a high-profile committee, wanting one with "star appeal and political intrigue."

## Turning bills into laws

Legislation starts with the introduction of a bill (from the medieval "bulla," a document with a seal). Representatives drop bills into a hopper—a mahogany box on the Speaker's rostrum—while senators hand theirs to the clerks at the dais in their chamber. Clerks assign the bill a number, and the parliamentarians refer it to the appropriate committee, as spelled out in the rules. In the Senate, a bill will be referred to only one committee; in the House, all or portions of the same bill might be referred to multiple committees.

As a senator for ten years, Harry Truman concluded that a legislator's greatest accomplishment was preventing bad ideas from getting passed, and indeed most bills die in committee. Of the fourteen thousand bills introduced during the 110th Congress (2007–2009), only 3.3 percent were enacted into law. Some members have introduced hundreds of bills in a single Congress, with no expectation of getting them passed. Instead, they see them as a way to study ideas, to promote personal interests and ideological aspirations, to help a constituent or a contributor, or to advance an economic interest important to their state.

To distinguish major bills from the mass being introduced every year, members will reserve symbolic numbers such as S1 or HR1776. They also devise elaborate titles with headline-friendly acronyms such as the USA PATRIOT Act, which stands for Uniting and Strengthening America by Providing Appropriate Tools Required to Intercept and Obstruct Terrorism. Signature achievements of congressional careers are bills that become known by their names, usually linking the chief Senate and House sponsors, such as the Taft-Hartley Act or the Sarbanes-Oxley Act.

To increase the chances of their bills being taken seriously, proponents will seek cosponsors by sending out "Dear Colleague" letters. The more compelling the legislation, the more co-sponsors it will attract and the more likely it is to pass. The bill creating the Vietnam Veterans Memorial got all one hundred senators as co-sponsors, guaranteeing its passage.

After sorting through the pile of bills referred to them, the chairs of the standing committees and subcommittees will decide what to take up, and in what order. Becoming chairman used to be determined strictly by seniority. Once members got on to a committee they advanced up the ladder by their length of service, no matter how far they strayed from their party's core positions. This eliminated the potential for conflict in selecting chairmen in general. For much of the twentieth century, chairmen acted as barons who ruled their committees in styles ranging from despotic to democratic. They decided when the committee would meet, whether it would have subcommittees, what issues it would take up, and who would serve on its staff. By the 1970s, reforms in both the House and Senate reduced the independent powers of the committee chairs, rewarding party loyalty over seniority and giving other committee members the ability to force an issue on the agenda, as well as more say over the staff.

In committee

Committee chairs still retain clout, particularly since it is the "chairman's mark," or the draft of a bill, that usually forms the starting point for committee deliberations. Despite their reduced powers, Senator Ernest Hollings (D-South Carolina) cautioned against falling out of favor with the committee chairs: "If a senator has introduced a bill and he wants to see it move, you can pretty much count on the fact that if he really goes after the chairman on some other issue, he's not going to get what he wants on his own bill." The role of the ranking member of the minority party on the committee is more problematic. The chairman "drives the car and chooses the destination," explained

Senator Bob Kerrey (D-Nebraska). "The ranking [member] rides shotgun on a good day. On a bad day, he or she is in a carpool with the chairman's staff."

Both parties used to relegate new senators to minor committees, letting them get seasoned in the minors before bringing them up to the majors. As Senate Democratic leader, Lyndon Johnson began the practice of putting every freshman in his conference on at least one prestigious committee from the start. Most freshmen now either chair or serve as ranking minority member of a subcommittee. This gives newcomers the opportunity to develop their own legislative voice, stake a claim on an issue, and build a platform for their causes (not to mention making them grateful to the leaders who bestowed the assignments). Leaders reasoned that freshmen would have more time to devote to their subcommittees and would welcome the responsibility. Spreading chairmanships also improved the visibility of the parties' rising stars. But these efforts also frustrated the periodic attempt to reduce the proliferating number of competing committees and subcommittees.

As the congressional workload increased, so did the number of standing committees, those that continue from one Congress to the next. The Legislative Reorganization Act of 1946 cut the number of committees, consolidated jurisdictions, and tried to reduce the redundancy of government officials giving the same testimony before separate House and Senate committees by fostering joint committees. But the natural disinclination of the two bodies to work in tandem has limited joint committees to such housekeeping issues as government printing and overseeing the Library of Congress. That reorganization act also established the first professional staffs for congressional committees. Previously, clerical duties had been handled by a few clerks, patronage appointees who were often family members of the chairman. During World War II, for instance, the Senate Foreign

Relations Committee's entire staff consisted of a secretary, a clerk, and a part-time assistant. When the United States emerged from the war, Congress recognized that the growth and complexity of the government would require more professional staff assistance (by the end of the twentieth century the committee's staff had topped fifty).

The first professional committee staffs were nonpartisan, assigned to work equally for the majority and the minority, and did not change when control of the chamber shifted between the parties. The same staff member might write the committee report for a bill and a statement in opposition. This system collapsed in the 1970s, after minority members complained that the staffs tended to reflect the chairmen's interests rather than theirs. Committees were authorized to hire minority staffs, which by default converted the professional staff into the majority staff. Committee staff took on much of the preliminary work in drafting bills, carrying out negotiations, preparing questions for members to ask during hearings, and briefing them on the progress of the legislation.

Committees call expert witnesses to testify, and they can subpoena reluctant witnesses and punish the uncooperative by charging them with contempt of Congress, which carries the possibility of a fine or imprisonment. A few officials have been threatened with impeachment for failing to provide information that committees requested. Most agency heads testify willingly, however, since they are likely seeking support for their programs from the same committees. In questioning these witnesses, senior members go first, while juniors patiently wait their turn. Committee members and staff know that the choice of witnesses can shape the form of the debate and the legislation it produces. "[If] you get the right witnesses and ask the right questions and they give the right answers," commented one committee clerk, "your opposition is slaughtered before they can open their trap."

From the subcommittee, the bill goes to the full committee, where members will review and revise it, section by section, in a markup session. During markups, compromises are forged, new items are added, and some provisions disappear entirely. The committee then reports the marked-up bill to the full House or Senate, with an accompanying report that explains the bill's provisions. Hearings and reports will be published to create a record, Congress prints the largest share of what it does, and today places much of it online.

Most bills pass in a form close to the way they emerged from committee, demonstrating that committee members have the largest say about what goes into the legislation. Members from both parties are attracted to particular committees because of their personal interest in the issues they handle, or because those issues impact their home states. Consequently, deliberations in committee have a less partisan tone than on the floor. On the Senate floor, proposed amendments may try to improve or sabotage the bill, but often there is not much left to add by the time the bill leaves the committee. The advantage of a committee bill, produced by the "regular order," is that it has gone through an exacting review that has achieved some common ground through negotiation. One senator recalled a bill that consumed six "tough and laborious" days of committee markups, with fifty-nine amendments that strengthened the measure.

Sometimes, party leaders will bypass a standing committee by appointing a special task force to draft the legislation. This procedure allows members who are committed to some issue to maneuver around committee obstacles, particularly when a sizeable majority in the chamber thinks differently than the majority of a committee. In the Senate, the problem with evading the regular order is that the bill can be bombarded with divisive amendments that a standing committee might have worked through in markup sessions. Opponents of special task forces interpret the leadership as saying: "We have this legislation we want to shove down your throat."

## House committees

The committee system is firmly entrenched in Congress. In 1789 the House and Senate appointed ad hoc committees that dealt with single issues and then disbanded. As the larger body, and thus in need of greater organization, the House created its first standing committee in the First Congress. Over the next quarter century it added twenty-five more. The smaller Senate relied on ad hoc committees until the bungled War of 1812 left the Capitol building in ruins and convinced senators of the need for greater stability, continuity, and expertise.

The rules of each house lay out the jurisdictions of their committees, but some issues do not fit so neatly and thus overlap. Since the House can make multiple referrals of parts of the same bill to several committees, two or more committees may oversee the same agency and may issue contradictory directives. House committees will engage in turf wars with each other that require some bargaining to make peace. Both the Energy and Commerce and the Judiciary committees, for instance, claimed the right to handle legislation to deregulate the broadband Internet market in 2001, and their conflict stalled the legislation. The Speaker had to order the committee chairs to negotiate with each other until they reached a compromise.

The Constitution stipulates that all revenue bills must originate in the House (Article I, section 7), which the House has interpreted to include all bills that raise and spend federal funds. The Ways and Means Committee was established in 1795 to have charge of both revenue and expenditures, until those functions were split by the creation of a separate Appropriations Committee in 1865. The House has made Ways and Means an "exclusive committee," meaning that its members do not serve on other committees (the Rules and Appropriations committees similarly require exclusive service). In addition to taxes and tariffs, Ways and Means holds

In committee

jurisdiction over Social Security and Medicare. Given such vast responsibilities, the parties have generally avoided appointing "bomb throwers" to the committee, trying to preserve an atmosphere of reasonable accommodation. Wilbur Mills (D-Arkansas), regarded as "the most powerful man in Washington" for his influence over tax policies during his chairmanship from 1957 to 1975, epitomized the committee's reputation for bipartisanship.

That image was shaken during the chairmanship of Bill Thomas (R-California). Having served for twenty-three years before becoming chairman, he grew impatient with the obstacles in the legislative process and those who invoked them. Wielding a heavy gavel, Chairman Thomas once summoned the Capitol police to eject minority members from a committee meeting. In 2006 Thomas insisted on bundling three separate tax initiatives into the same bill, which he called a "trifecta" (after the pari-mutuel bet that calls the first three horses in order). Senator Charles Grassley (R-Iowa), who chaired the Finance Committee, pointed out that the odds against "trifecta" bets were astronomical. Grassley calculated that the Senate would likely pass two of the tax measures, but not the third, and urged that they be voted on separately. Thomas prevailed in conference, but as Grassley predicted, the entire tax package went down to defeat, contributing to the charges of a "do-nothing" Congress.

## Senate committees

Congressional power in the Gilded Age of the late nineteenth century was concentrated in the committee chairmen of both the House and Senate. They occupied handsome committee rooms in the Capitol, outfitted with rolltop desks, plush leather chairs, chaise lounges, carved sideboards, Turkish rugs, and French beveled mirrors. The committee room served as a private office for the chairman, who could also hire a clerk. The importance of the legislation that a committee handled determined its room's proximity to the House and Senate chambers, with the "money"

committees—Appropriations, Finance, and Ways and Means—
situated closest to the chambers. In the Senate, most committees
were sinecures that existed solely to give the chairman a room and a
clerk, and never handled any legislation. A few sinecure committees
even went to senior members of the minority party, indicating
the shallowness of the majority's interest in the issue (one was the
committee on woman suffrage). Not until the first congressional
office building opened in 1908 and 1909 did all members get
individual offices. After that, the Senate trimmed its seventy-five
committees down to the twenty that actually handled legislation.

During the half century between the elections of 1932 and 1980,
Senate Democrats held the majority in all but two Congresses,
and southerners chaired the most influential committees. The
one-party "Solid South" regularly reelected senators to allow them
to gain seniority. More conservative than the national Democratic
Party, they often stood as obstacles to liberal reforms—notably
Representative Howard W. Smith (D-Virginia), who chaired the
Rules Committee from 1955 to 1967, and Senator James Eastland
(D-Mississippi), who chaired the Judiciary Committee from
1955 to 1977, both of whom tried to stymie civil rights legislation.
Eastland's intransigence forced the Democratic leadership to
bring civil rights legislation directly to the floor and bypass
his committee. Chairman Eastland ran the full committee as a
fiefdom, and just as feudal lords bound their vassals by mutual ties
of service and protection, he was shrewd enough to grant its more
liberal members relative autonomy within their subcommittees.

Senators, like representatives, are drawn to committees because
of common interests. Members of the Agriculture Committee may
represent wheat, corn, cotton, tobacco, sugar, or dairy producing
states, but they share mutual concerns over farm subsidies,
international trade, and emergency relief. Those who serve on
the Armed Services Committee tend to favor a strong national
defense, while those on the Senate Foreign Relations and House
Foreign Affairs committees put greater faith in diplomacy.

5. Senator Edward M. Kennedy (D-Massachusetts) chairs a hearing of the Senate Judiciary Committee. He is flanked by Senators Howard Metzenbaum (D-Ohio) and Strom Thurmond (R-South Carolina).

Members of these committees may be little known outside of their home states and may devote themselves to legislative work rather than seek the national spotlight, trying to accomplish much with a minimum of disruption. Some committees are more polarized, notably the Judiciary Committee, when both parties appoint reliable ideological warriors who battle over the courts, constitutional amendments, and civil liberties. Senators once voted for qualified judicial nominations regardless of ideology, out of deference to the president, but over time the confirmation process developed into a battle of wills between presidents and the Senate, as the federal judiciary took a more active role in policy making by interpreting the laws beyond what some members of Congress believed they had intended.

Because senators serve on more committees than do representatives, they are more generalists than specialists—House members accuse senators of being willing to talk to the media

about any subject. The difference between the two bodies becomes particularly evident when they meet in conference committees, where representatives may be better versed in legislative details and need to rely less on staff.

## Appropriations: where things happen

A freshman senator once asked Senator Richard Russell for help in getting appointed to the Armed Services Committee, which Russell chaired. Russell counseled against it, explaining that Congress was not like a state legislature, where the same committee authorized a program and approved the money to pay for it. In the Senate, after an authorizing committee held its hearings on an issue, the Appropriations Committee would hold its own hearing and then appropriate whatever it decided, more or less or nothing at all. "What you want is a seat on the Appropriations Committee," Russell advised, "where things happen."

The congressional power of the purse, covering all federal funds, is the central legislative function (Article I, section 9). Appropriations are made annually, and bills are due for the president's signature by October 1. Congress rarely meets this deadline, however, and often passes a continuing resolution (CR) to maintain spending at the previous year's levels. Although not the best way to fund government operations, since it does not meet changing needs, a CR at least buys Congress additional time. Congress will sometimes bundle appropriations bills into omnibus measures that combine funding for several agencies into one package, with something for everyone. Supplemental appropriations will also cover unexpected expenses, such as disaster relief.

Today, the largest part of the budget goes to such mandatory programs (called entitlements) as Social Security, Medicare, and veterans' pensions, and to defense spending. A smaller portion of the budget funds the rest of government programs and expenses. The standing committees can authorize new projects, but those projects cannot get under way until funds have been appropriated to pay for them. The early nineteenth-century House and Senate operated without Appropriations committees, but the authorizing committees naturally wanted to fund all of the projects they passed, making apparent the need for gate-keeping Appropriations committees. To better manage the process, Congress created the Budget Bureau (now the Office of Management and Budget) in 1921 and established Budget committees in 1975.

Early each year, after the president sends a budget to Congress, the nonpartisan Congressional Budget Office reviews it and prepares its own estimates of expenditures and revenues. The Budget committees then hold hearings, allowing the administration to make its case, along with a few outside witnesses. Their analysts scour the president's budget, line by line, make adjustments, and draft the budget resolution. The president typically threatens to veto anything that exceeds his budget requests. Members negotiate their differences in markup sessions, and the budget resolution they produce will serve as a blueprint of government finances for the coming year, calculating how much revenue will be taken in, the anticipated costs of entitlements, and the remaining levels of appropriations. If the budget resolution has not been passed by April 15, the Appropriation subcommittees can begin their work without a resolution, motivating the Budget committees to finish in time.

A provision in the Budget Act called reconciliation enabled the Budget committees to order other committees to reconcile their spending figures with the budget, whether tax bills, entitlement spending, or direct spending. Reconciliation provided a significant procedural breakthrough because it set a time limit on how long the budget bills could be debated, so they could not be filibustered in the Senate. Because of this provision, any changes in taxes or entitlements will usually appear under the title "Budget

and Reconciliation Act of" a particular year. The House's rules restrict amendments, and senators are limited to fifty hours of debate. Even after the fifty hours, senators can continue to offer amendments, but they will have no time to debate them. To dispose of the abundance of amendments that are usually offered, the Senate holds "vote-a-ramas," taking one vote after another, throughout the day and into the night, unless the sponsors withdraw their amendments. Originally designed to reconcile differences between the congressional Budget and Appropriations committees, reconciliation's ability to dodge filibusters made it an attractive legislative tactic to push controversial legislation through the Senate. In 1981, Senate Republicans led by Howard Baker (R-Tennessee) employed reconciliation to enact President Ronald Reagan's massive tax cuts. Many senators objected, however, and the Senate later added a provision that measures passed by reconciliation could not increase the federal deficit.

The budget determines how much money the Appropriations committees can distribute. They divide that amount among their dozen subcommittees, which will each appropriate every penny of their allotment. Subcommittees oversee specific areas of federal spending—such as agriculture, defense, state and foreign operations, and energy—and enjoy such prestige and authority that their chairs have been dubbed the "cardinals" of Capitol Hill. Since it is hard for members outside the Appropriations Committee to add amendments, committee members are buttonholed on the House and Senate floor by those seeking funding for a pet project.

Appropriations subcommittees on the Senate side must wait for their House counterparts to act first, which gives the House Appropriations Committee a weightier role in the appropriations process. Its larger staff will draft the original bills and conference reports. Since senators can amend the spending priorities set by the House, they serve as a court of appeals for those agencies and private interests that feel that the House committee slighted them.

**6. The Senate and House pass their own versions of all appropriations bills and then meet in conference committee to resolve their differences, as seen in this conference in the 1970s.**

Senate subcommittees sometimes hold hearings and draft a bill first, but if the House feels that the Senate has overstepped its authority it will "blue slip" the appropriation. The House returns the Senate bill attached to a resolution of disapproval that is printed on a blue slip of paper, hence the expression. On other occasions, the House finds it expedient to look the other way. When facing massive budget deficits in 1982, for instance, the Senate hiked taxes significantly by amending a revenue bill in which the House had actually lowered taxes.

In both bodies, the rules prohibit members from trying to legislate on an appropriations bill, that is, authorizing new programs on bills that appropriate the money to fund them. This has not stopped senators from seeking to inject legislative goals into the popular "must-pass" appropriations. When the presiding officer ruled one such amendment out of order, its sponsor appealed and

a majority vote overturned the ruling. For the next four years, that precedent allowed senators to legislate on appropriations bills, in spite of the prohibition against it in the rules. Majority Leader Trent Lott (R-Mississippi) finally arranged another vote to overturn the precedent and return to the rules. "I learned painfully what a mistake that was," Lott explained. "We should not be legislating on appropriations bills."

The Senate invariably amends House appropriations, requiring a conference committee to resolve the differences. The House Appropriations Committee expects all of its conferees to participate, whereas senators, other than the chair and ranking minority member, usually come and go. The large House contingent can exert an element of intimidation, but the senators can simply say: "This is the Senate's position. We're not yielding." Without some accommodation, the bill will not pass.

The House will then vote on the conference report, accepting it, rejecting it, or recommitting it to the conference for further consideration. Once the House adopts the measure, the conference committee is disbanded, and the Senate must either accept or reject the report. Once passed, the appropriations bill goes to the president, who has ten days to sign or veto it. If vetoed, it returns to Congress, which can revise it or attempt an override. Vetoing appropriations is a tricky business, since these thick bills will contain items that are high on the president's list of priorities. But since members of Congress also have a large stake in the bill, they will also be under pressure to meet the president's objections.

The appropriations process at times resembles a game of chicken, with the president and Congress driving head on toward each other, to see who swerves first. In 1995, President Bill Clinton vetoed several appropriations bills. The Republican majority in Congress could have passed a continuing resolution for continuity of government operations under the previous spending levels but chose instead to let the federal government shut down for lack of funds. The majority believed that the public would blame the president. To their surprise, the public disapproved the disruption of government services and faulted Congress instead.

Appropriations bills can provide a lump sum of operating funds to an agency or can instruct the agency exactly how to spend the money, by specific requests that have come to be known as earmarks. Earmarking has fallen into general disfavor, because of the lobbying surrounding them, but many members defend the practice on the grounds that the people's elected representatives, rather than bureaucrats, should determine federal spending. Initially, earmarks went mostly to research projects at universities. Between 1996 and 2006, however, the number of earmarks jumped from three thousand to thirteen thousand a session. Mayors began imploring their home-state delegations for federal funds for roads, sewerage treatment plants, harbor dredging, and environmental projects that were not high on the executive branch's list of objectives. Other earmarks reflected backdoor requests from executive branch agencies whose budget initiatives had been rejected by the Office of Management and Budget. Divided government fanned the practice when Congress became distrustful of the administration's spending priorities, particularly in the areas of defense and intelligence. But even after the majority and the president came from the same party, earmarks grew at a fast pace. Excesses drew public attention, symbolized by a $223 million appropriation in 2005 for a "bridge to nowhere" between two sparsely populated Alaskan communities.

Lobbyists saw earmarks as the most direct way of satisfying their clients' needs and worked to convince members of Congress of the value of the projects and the boost they would give their chances of reelection. Lobbyists who solicited earmarks also raised campaign funds, leaving the impression of a conflict of interest. After influence-peddling scandals surfaced in 2006, revealing that several members and staff had accepted favors in return for promoting earmarks, the practice became publicly equated with unsavory political machinations. Yet, public opinion on earmarks has been contradictory, with voters still expecting their own members to "bring home the bacon." One representative who issued a statement announcing that he had secured millions of federal dollars for projects in his district felt compelled to add: "There is a lot of talk about earmarks lately, and while I do not support wasteful spending, I do believe that members of Congress have better judgment as to the needs of their districts than some bureaucrat in Washington, D.C."

When he was a senator, John F. Kennedy chaired a committee to choose five outstanding U.S. senators to have their portraits displayed in the Reception Room outside the Senate chamber. As the top criteria, Kennedy cited acts of statesmanship that transcended state and party lines. This ideal seems the very opposite of "pork," and yet one of the five outstanding senators selected was Henry Clay (the others were Daniel Webster, John C. Calhoun, Robert La Follette [R-Wisconsin], and Robert Taft [R-Ohio]). During the antebellum period, Clay had promoted nationalism through federal support for such "internal improvements" as road building, canal digging, and harbor dredging. Clay's program built political coalitions in Congress while at the same time it sought to link the states in a national transportation network. Funding local projects has continued to be an essential ingredient in decision making within such a diverse democratic institution as Congress. More than a century later, Representative Bud Schuster (R-Pennsylvania) chaired the House Transportation and Infrastructure Committee, which produced legislation on highway and airport construction across the country. Schuster encouraged the expansion of his committee to seventy-five members—the largest in the House—reasoning that the more members who had a project in a bill, the more votes it would get on the floor. When his critics called spending on public works in someone else's back yard a pork barrel project, Schuster rebutted: "The one thing Congress is doing, over their objections, is building assets for the future of our country."

# Chapter 4
# **On the floor**

Following a decade in the House, Paul Simon (D-Illinois) won election to the Senate, whose differences in operation suited him perfectly. He regarded the House as the more committee-driven body, where members were discouraged from proposing bills outside the jurisdictions of the committees on which they served. His efforts to sponsor legislation beyond his own committees had usually been met with a dismissive, "We're looking into that," by the other committees' chairmen. By contrast, there were virtually no limitations on the subject of amendments a senator could offer to any bill being debated. With his wide range of interests, Simon could now "stick my toe into a number of bodies of water."

The differences between what happens on the floor of the more structured House and individualistic Senate are therefore critical for understanding the legislative process, and yet the visitors to the galleries of both chambers often come away baffled by what they have witnessed. They may see a speaker addressing an almost empty chamber as if surrounded by attentive colleagues, or nothing at all may be going on during a seemingly endless quorum call. The floor managers and opponents of a bill may be using impenetrable parliamentary language. Those who had hoped to hear a modern-day Daniel Webster will usually be disappointed, but occasionally a real debate will break out between opposing sides that know the subject intimately and dispute each other passionately. Then when the bells ring, the floor will become a kaleidoscope of activity, with members swirling in and out of different doors, casting votes and clustering together in small groups to swap stories or try to cut a deal.

Amid the oratory and activity that takes place on the floor, intricate legislative strategies are being tailored to aid a bill's enactment. Opposing sides will tap a range of parliamentary tactics to advance or derail the bill. Since party discipline has been historically difficult to enforce in Congress, bipartisan coalitions will be constructed around major bills, with each party seeking to pick off dissidents in the other, making the outcome of many legislative battles unpredictable.

## Debate, rules, and procedure

The floor proceedings in the House and Senate are a mix of procedure, policy, politics, personality, and posturing. Each day's session opens with a period of "morning business" when members make short speeches (one minute in the House, up to an hour in the Senate) on anything they wish, without rebuttal. After morning business the chambers take up legislation, and the debate can grow fiery, although the strict time limits in the House and the rules and traditions of the Senate generally preserve decorum. They may deliver their remarks to a largely empty chamber, or colloquies can take place between supporters or opponents on an issue. Reporters of debate record their words for publication in the next day's *Congressional Record*, defining a "true statesman" as someone who hands them a prepared text in advance.

In debate, the House maintains a five-minute rule limiting how long members can speak, although after it adjourns some members return under "special orders" to deliver lengthy speeches, where they "debate" an issue without the other side being present. Although they are not legislative sessions, special orders are still reported in the *Congressional Record* and broadcast over C-SPAN, and they can help members hone their talking points and obtain publicity. Before the cameras were installed in 1979, House members built their reputations largely in the committee rooms, but television allows them to address viewers across the nation. One representative who made frequent use of special orders noted that whenever he went on camera "the phones in my office would light up." Television particularly helps mavericks and minority parties that may lack the votes in Congress to enact their programs but can make a case for their alternatives to a national audience.

During his short stay in the Senate, Barack Obama (D-Illinois) spent little time on the Senate floor, rushing in primarily to cast a vote and then leaving for other pressing business. On those occasions when he presided, there would usually be only a single senator on the floor speaking to a nearly empty chamber. "In the world's greatest deliberative body," he noted, "no one is listening." Modern debate may not reach the heights of Daniel Webster and Henry Clay, and stump speaking went out long ago, but floor strategies depend more on votes than oratory. Gadflies who relish making sarcastic attacks in debate while in the minority will switch to pacifying, flattering, and trading with other members to support their bills once they get into the majority. Some of the most productive legislators rarely speak out. If they have the votes, they don't need a speech, they assume; if they need the speech, they don't have the votes. Occasionally, a speech may affect a bill's chances. Senator Harry Reid recalled that when he gave his maiden speech, proposing a taxpayers' bill of rights (a bill that he had never been able to get out of subcommittee while a member of the House), both the presiding officer and the senator waiting to speak next happened to be members of the Senate Finance Committee, which had jurisdiction over taxes. They heard him and agreed to help his bill. It passed, he commented, "not because of my ability to communicate as much as who was listening."

Congress does more business in public view than either of the other branches, and it publishes most of it as well, in hearing transcripts, reports, and other Senate and House documents. Almost everything that the members say, and some things that they did not say, appears in the next day's *Congressional Record*. The Constitution does not require Congress to do its business in public or to publish its entire proceedings, only to publish a journal "from time to time." The House and Senate keep journals of their proceedings that are summaries of the day's activities. These are different from the *Congressional Record*, which evolved from notes taken by early newspaper reporters for publication in their papers that were later compiled as the *Annals of Debate, Register of Debate*, and the *Congressional Globe*. Congress did not hire official reporters of debate until the 1840s, and the Government Printing Office did not begin publishing the *Congressional Record* until 1872. The daily *Record* is a grab bag of information that includes not only the text of bills, and speeches about them, but editorials, eulogies, commencement addresses, letters from constituents, and a host of other items that members insert to show what they are reading and thinking.

Among the handful of members in either chamber at any given time, waiting their turn to speak, one has been tapped by the Speaker or the president pro tem to preside on a rotating basis. Some regard it as an onerous duty, but presiding is the best means for members to familiarize themselves with the proceedings and the rules. They can also earn some chits with their colleagues by agreeing to preside for them. The greenest presiding officer need only follow the advice (and repeat aloud the words the parliamentarian has whispered), but when the proceedings turn contentious, more experienced members will take the chair.

The House and Senate parliamentarians must master not only the formal rules but thousands of precedents as well. Knowledgeable, impartial, and discreet, parliamentarians offer information to both sides in a debate, and they avoid divulging confidences from one side to the other by answering *only* the questions they are asked. The House is more structured in its procedure than the Senate, but both bodies can relax or even suspend their rules. The House does this by shifting into a "committee of the whole," where looser rules expedite business (the Senate operates as a committee of the whole only as a court of impeachment). The Senate instead uses unanimous consent requests to relax or suspend its rules. Eugene J. McCarthy (D-Minnesota), who served in both bodies, took a cynical attitude toward their rules and procedures, and advised new members against spending much time trying to learn them. "The Senate rules are simple enough to learn, but they are seldom honored in practice," McCarthy observed. "House rules are too complicated. Use the parliamentarian."

## Majority rule in the House

It is when the majority leader calls a major bill off the legislative calendar (the list of bills reported from committee and ready to be debated and voted on) that the House and the Senate operate most differently. In the House, the bill goes first to the Rules Committee, which is firmly under the control of the majority party and which will draft a resolution known as a special rule, or special order of business, that sets the number and type of amendments to be offered on the floor and the time allotted for debate. Once the House has passed the special rule by majority vote, the majority leader knows that so long as the majority remains united, it will have the votes to pass the legislation. The minority can do little other than try to bait the majority. "There are times, I can tell my colleagues without any reservation, when I wish I were the Speaker of the House," a Senate majority leader said wistfully. "The Speaker of the House doesn't have to worry about the minority, they run over everybody."

Given its size and inherent unwieldiness, the House does not permit filibusters and other delaying tactics. Its rules make it easier to shut off debate and force a vote. Majority parties in

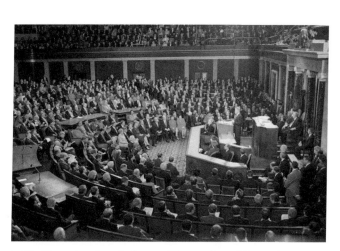

7. The House chamber, the larger of the two, hosts joint sessions of the House and Senate.

the House have adopted various strategies, from allowing a large number of amendments (to accommodate divisions in the party) to restricting the number that can be debated (to force party unity). Whenever a party has held a large majority, it has not been unusual for the House to debate many amendments on major bills, such as defense authorizations. "It was easy to be magnanimous and allow minority amendments with a sizeable majority that doomed them," noted one House staffer. But narrower margins make the outcome uncertain, causing the majority party to restrict efforts to offer amendments.

"Saving" amendments may be introduced if the bill is in trouble and needs help. In 1968, Representative Charles Mathias (R-Maryland) supported an open housing bill that banned racial discrimination in selling and renting homes. He offered a "saving amendment" that weakened one section of the bill in order to prevent its opponents from defeating it entirely. By contrast, "killer" amendments are designed to scare off support by making the bill unpalatable. Killer amendments can backfire, however, as when Representative Howard Smith, a segregationist, sought to defeat the Civil Rights Act of 1964 by adding a provision for equal rights for women. Liberals worried that the amendment would undermine support for the bill as a whole, but accepted it, and the landmark women's rights provisions became law. When congratulated on its passage, a chagrined Smith replied, "Well, of course, you know, I offered it as a joke."

The opposition may introduce an amendment that is unrelated to the subject of the bill, just to provoke a fight. If the chair rules the amendment out of order, the opponents can make a motion to overrule the chair, setting up a further vote to table the appeal. Even though the minority knows it will lose, it can force vulnerable members from swing districts to go on record on issues that might jeopardize their reelections, even when voting on procedural rather than substantive motions. Amendments dealing with taxes, for instance, can produce negative ads in the next election.

The House Rules Committee may add a "self-executing" amendment to the bill, replacing provisions from the original bill with its own ideas. The Rules Committee will then stipulate that its amendment will be adopted as soon as the House votes for the special rule calling the bill for debate. This procedure was originally used to make technical corrections to a bill, but over time the majority leadership has invoked it to circumvent the committees and make substantive changes in the legislation.

Generally speaking, the majority will not do anything to help the minority; however, when House Republicans returned to power in 1995, they did away with a provision that had irked them during their four decades in the minority. They prohibited the Rules Committee from reporting any special rule that denied the minority the chance to make a "motion to recommit with instructions." This procedural motion allowed opponents to delay a bill by sending it back to committee. Since a motion to recommit could be amended, it also gave the minority an opportunity to offer amendments on the floor. Returning a bill to committee did not necessarily kill it (the committee could report it out again), but since the bill had already consumed precious time on the floor, the majority leader would probably not be anxious to call it back up.

But having handed their opponents a weapon, in the motion to recommit, the majority party still had ways of disarming the minority. Republican majority leaders instructed their conference members to vote against Democratic motions to recommit, no matter what the issue. Such party unity was less common in the Democratic conference, so when Democrats returned to the majority, they rewrote the rules to limit the use of motions to recommit. The majority can also counter the minority's motions by bringing up a bill under a "suspension of the rules," a procedural matter to expedite business on such noncontroversial matters as naming a post office, and which requires a two-thirds vote to pass. Calling up a major bill on the suspension calendar is therefore a gamble, likely to lead to defeat. Even so, since suspension bills cannot be amended, the maneuver prevents members of the minority from offering amendments that could embarrass the majority. The majority thus protects itself, although it may not have advanced its legislative agenda.

Votes may pit members' party loyalty against their popularity at home. Party leaders know that it is self-defeating to ask members to commit political suicide, and they grant leeway in matters of state interest. But every vote can be critical. "Jeez, Tip, that's a hard one," Joe Moakley (D-Massachusetts) once demurred when his colleague Speaker Thomas P. "Tip" O'Neill (D-Massachusetts) pressed for his support on a critical vote in the House Rules Committee. "Hey, Josie," O'Neill replied, "I don't need you on the easy ones."

The House majority usually prevails, but not always. On some occasions, the Speaker and majority leader have felt pressure to let bills that they oppose go to the floor for a vote. After President George W. Bush vetoed an Iraq war spending bill that included a timetable for withdrawing American troops, Speaker Nancy Pelosi, who supported a timetable, allowed a vote on a revised bill without one because she knew the majority lacked the two-thirds vote needed to override the presidential veto. To make the bill more palatable to their conference, Democratic leaders added other measures, including raising the minimum wage and providing disaster relief for Hurricane Katrina victims. This version passed and got the president's signature.

The House is famous for the rough and tumble of its floor proceedings, and some fierce battles have been fought there throughout history. Political scientists who have studied the proceedings note that while comity and cooperation would always be welcome, real legislative achievement has come through political stamina and persistence. Representatives argue that conflict is an integral part of governing, that their differences of opinion reflect the diversity of views in the country, and that even angry debate can produce legislation and reform. "Many observers think our zeal and partisanship too childish, that much too often we disingenuously posture for partisan gain," Sherrod Brown (D-Ohio) commented on his House service. "But these displays of passion and anger, and even the barbs, are rhetorical outlets for those same deeply held beliefs." After all, members got to Congress by waging campaigns in which they were targets of attack from opponents and editorial writers. Usually, they are well equipped to handle themselves in legislative battle on the House floor.

## Minority muscle in the Senate

Representatives who get elected to the Senate need to forget most of what they learned about the rules of the House, since the two operate so differently. There is little compulsion in the Senate, whose schedule and procedures are whatever the leadership can work out. The Senate is more courtly and deliberate in its pace of business, and more accommodating of each of its members, doing the bulk of its business by unanimous consent. That means that a single member can hold up business in the Senate, making it a personality-driven institution. House leaders frequently call on their Senate counterparts to show some backbone and stand up to the opposition, but Senate leaders respond that they simply do not have the same legislative and procedural strength and power as the House.

The Senate requires a quorum of 51 percent of its members in order to do business, but there are usually few senators on the floor, except during a vote. A quorum is always assumed to be present, unless a senator calls attention to the absence of a quorum as a delaying tactic. A majority is then needed to establish a quorum so the proceedings can continue. Bells are rung to summon the senators to answer the roll. On occasion, senators have deliberately avoided going to the chamber in order, to keep the majority from acting. The majority leader can then instruct the sergeant at arms to "arrest" the absent members and escort them to the chamber, even carry them in physically. Most of the time, however, quorum calls are simply a device to keep the chamber in session while a compromise amendment is being drafted in the cloakrooms, or when the next scheduled speaker is late arriving, a procedure that is less cumbersome than a formal recess.

Senators sit at assigned desks in the chamber. Each morning a squad of high-school-age pages neatly stack on each senator's desk the previous day's *Congressional Record* and the most recent executive calendar (listing upcoming nominations and treaties) and legislative calendar (the "Calendar of Business" that lists pending bills and resolutions), along with bills to be debated that day or the conference report. This neatness can be deceiving, since the proceedings will be anything but orderly. The Senate passes hundreds of bills over the year but debates only a few dozen of them. The vast majority of bills and resolutions pass by unanimous consent agreements or voice votes, without protracted debate and roll calls. Agreements are worked out in the committees and cloakrooms, narrowing the areas of contention requiring floor fights. But many votes will still be held, requiring the party leaders to stay close by at all times. Senator Mitch McConnell (R-Kentucky), who served as whip and floor leader, emphasized the importance of spending time on the floor and being there when "you've got a tough, close vote." Among the senators filing into the chamber, some of them may be urged to vote one way by their staffs but will remain open to reason from their party leaders.

Unlike the House, whose Rules Committee determines the fate of major bills on the House floor, the Senate Rules and Administration Committee assigns office space and parking space, valuable commodities that have little to do with moving legislation. Without the benefit of the special rules enjoyed by their House counterparts, Senate leaders have relied instead on unanimous consent (UC) agreements. A UC might cover such routine business as asking that a speech be printed in the *Congressional Record* as if it had been delivered in full, or it might define how long a bill is debated and how it is amended. A UC can also pass an entire bill, without debate or a roll-call vote. The more complex agreements are painstakingly constructed in negotiations between the party floor leaders and once adopted can be changed only by unanimous consent.

The Senate now does the bulk of its business by unanimous consent. Such agreements can suspend the regular rules to save time. For instance, the Senate has a rule requiring that a bill have three readings before passage, which is routinely suspended by UC, unless a senator wants to delay action and objects, forcing the clerks to spend hours reading hundreds of pages of text aloud. The UC helps the leadership move legislation while simultaneously empowering every senator, any one of whom can stand and say "I object." The leadership will then try to determine

"SENATORIAL COURTESY."

8. This cartoon, which appeared in *Puck* on October 18, 1893, spoofed the Senate's tradition of unlimited debate, indicating that excessive oratory might not be persuasive.

the cause of the objection (which may or may not have anything to do with the matter being considered) and decide whether they can meet it.

The flip side of the UC is the "hold." Senators privately inform their party leaders that they are placing a hold on a bill or nomination. The majority leader will then not call up the matter for consideration until the hold has been lifted. Nowhere do the Senate rules authorize holds, but the practice has been honored because party leaders, not wanting to be blindsided, want to know if someone plans to object to a UC. Members may lift holds if their objections are met, or the majority leader may wait until the end of a session and let it be known that all holds are off, to test whether the objections have faded.

A single senator can thwart the will of the Senate, the House, and the president. On the last night before the summer recess in 1988, the Senate debated a bill to repeal the law that separated banks from stock brokerages. Both houses had passed the bill overwhelmingly, but not in the same form. A conference report resolved the differences, and the House approved it. When the Senate finally took it up, the chairman of the Senate Banking Committee asked for unanimous consent to dispense with the lengthy reading of the bill. A lone dissenter, Alphonse D'Amato (R-New York), objected, repeatedly. "The senator has something wrong with his hearing," he said after another unanimous consent agreement had been requested. "I object. If you want me to do it louder, I will do it louder." Since most of the senators had already departed for home, leaving only the committee members behind, there was no way to adopt the conference report by roll call, and D'Amato made unanimous consent impossible. So the Senate adjourned without passing the bill.

Because votes in the Senate are often close, accompanied by intense courting of the last undecided votes on controversial issue, fence sitters wield considerable leverage in dealing with the bill's managers. Senators are courted by local interests, lobbyists, administration liaisons, and others who seek their help and their vote. More than one majority leader has compared trying to lead a body of such strong individuals to herding cats. Senate rules assign few specific powers to the majority leader. Lyndon Johnson (D-Texas) once commented that he had only the power of persuasion to reply upon. Other leaders have described the Senate as a "complex web of relationships" among a hundred individuals from different states, different experiences, and different points of view.

Since 1975, when cloture was reduced from two-thirds to three-fifths of the Senate (sixty of the one hundred senators), majority leaders have increasingly filed cloture motions to limit debate as soon as they call up major bills. The majority leader makes a motion to proceed to a bill, and because that motion is debatable, the leader immediately files a cloture motion. Achieving cloture demonstrates that the Senate is serious about the bill and will pass some form of it. If the cloture motion fails, the majority leader will take up another issue for the time being.

With senators commuting to their home states each weekend, the legislative work week has been reduced to Tuesday through Thursday. The condensed time to get anything done has made the threat of filibuster more potent. Instead of the old-fashioned way of senators doing a lot of talking, the filibuster has become a silent tool for the minority and has become a regular occurrence rather than a weapon of last resort. "The cost of a filibuster today is very cheap," commented Senator Arlen Specter. "All you have to do is say: I am going to filibuster. Then there is a cloture vote, and sixty votes are not obtained, and the issue goes away." For all its headaches, the sixty-vote requirement to do business forces compromise and bipartisanship. To get anything of consequence done, senators must reach across party lines and attract broad support that spans party, region, and ideology.

In the 1970s, Senator Jesse Helms (R-North Carolina) pioneered the tactic of repeatedly proposing controversial amendments and demanding roll-call votes, even though his side would likely lose. The conservative Helms aimed to put liberal lawmakers on record on such social issues as AIDS funding, abortion, court-ordered school busing, and federal financing of the sometimes tasteless arts. "I wanted senators to take stands and do it publicly. I was willing to leave it to their constituents to decide what would happen next," Helms said, defending his actions. "When senators had to run on their record instead of their rhetoric, things really began to change."

To counteract such tactics, majority leaders have resorted to "filling the amendment tree." Normally, senators lose the floor as soon as they file an amendment, but under the "right of first recognition" the majority leader is always called on before anyone else. Therefore the majority leader can file an amendment and immediately seek recognition to add an amendment to the amendment (known as a "second-degree amendment"), and keep on filing amendments. Until the Senate votes on these amendments, no other amendments will be in order. A diagram of how such amendments branch out resembles a tree, so they are called "amendment trees." The objective is to prevent opponents of the bill from securing the first vote on an amendment of their choosing, perhaps something that would create political problems for the majority or would significantly alter the bill.

Minority members protest that filling the amendment tree precludes meaningful debate. They can no longer simply come to the floor and offer amendments. One senator tried to interest the press in his resolution banning senators from offering a second-degree amendment to their own amendments. Reporters in the press gallery had to advise him that no story was likely to appear because "it couldn't be explained to anybody beyond the Beltway."

## Making laws and making sausage

"Laws are like sausages," goes an old saying. "It is better not to see them being made." A mix of persuasion, pressure, and bargaining will be ground into every bill that becomes law. Managing legislation through to enactment involves finding something to offer to as many members as possible. On those where they have little stake, members may trade votes, supporting someone else's pet project in return for a promise of support on theirs, a practice called logrolling. Members will feel pressure from the president, their party, their constituents, and lobbyists on how to vote. Some will not make up their minds until the last minute, on the way to cast their vote. They have compared this situation to a "seminar on the run," as they try to determine how to vote from notes stuffed in their pockets, briefing books, whispers from staff, hurried briefings from colleagues, and last-minute calls from the White House.

The number of roll-call votes has accelerated. In 1953, the first year of the Eisenhower administration, the House held 71 recorded votes, and the Senate 89. By 1999, recorded votes in the House had risen to 611 and in the Senate to 374, reflecting changes in procedures that made it easier to offer amendments and gain recorded votes.

Anxious to know the probable outcome of a vote, party leaders deploy their whips to serve as "head counters." In the House, deputy and regional whips will determine how members are leaning and then stand in the doorways to the chamber to encourage members to vote with the party. "If you really are a good vote-counter, you don't let something come up that you can't win," said a former House majority whip, Tony Coehlo (D-California). Good vote-counters save information about the members and use it to trade, cajole, lean on, and threaten them. Torn between their desire to stand with their party and "vote their district," members can be deliberately unclear about their intentions. Unless vote-counters are good at recognizing body language, they may mistakenly put down a yes vote for someone who may be undecided or even a "no."

Vote counters warn that it is dangerous to assume anyone's support. Party, ideology, and personal factors may influence a member's vote. Once, Senator Roman Hruska (R-Nebraska) took it for granted that Barry Goldwater (R-Arizona), a fellow conservative, would support the voting rights bill he was sponsoring, without realizing that Goldwater had placed an amendment on the liberal alternative version of the bill. Stunned when Goldwater voted against him, Hruska rushed over to demand an explanation. "I've got an amendment in that bill," Goldwater explained, "and I'm not going to vote against my own amendment."

It generally takes fifteen to twenty minutes for the Senate and House to vote. During that time, members can switch their votes, leading to some intense appeals from anxious party leaders and colleagues if the vote is especially close. Or the leadership may hold some votes in reserve and free them to make a more politically expedient vote once it becomes clear that the measure will pass without them. In the Senate, the legislative clerk reads aloud those who voted in the affirmative and negative, and hands the final tally to the presiding officer to declare the measure passed or failed. In the House, with its electronic voting, votes have sometimes changed on the scoreboard after the presiding officer has gaveled the vote to a close. In fact, the sound of the gavel hitting the desk does not signal the official end of a vote. No House vote is official until the presiding officer announces the results of the voting sheets prepared by tally clerks.

Even after both houses have passed the bill, the process is not over. If the two versions differ, one body must accept the other's changes, or else they will hold further negotiations in a conference committee. The variations may be staggering. The farm bill that the House passed on July 27, 2007, for instance, was 160 pages long. The version that the Senate passed on December 14 was 1,876 pages. It took months of additional dickering to reconcile the two.

After one house has voted on a bill, those interests that are dissatisfied with that version will appeal to the other house, seeking specific changes. If the second body incorporates these changes into its bill, it gains broader support. Consequently, when House and Senate conferees meet to iron out their differences, the final bill will more closely resemble the second version.

The legislative strategy between the two houses sometimes requires a face-saving distraction. In the early 1950s, the Senate repeatedly passed legislation for federal aid to education that did not clear the House. Then in 1958, the Soviet Union shocked Congress and the public by launching the first Earth satellite, *Sputnik*. In response, the Senate renamed its bill the National Defense Education Act, emphasizing science education to help Americans catch up with the Soviets. The bill still faced skepticism in the House, so the chairman of the House subcommittee on education, Carl Elliot (D-Alabama) framed the debate in the House in terms of awarding the scholarships as loans, whereas the Senate had advocated making them grants. House members denounced grants as a form of socialism. "And the minute the damn scholarship issue was done for, dead, the bill swooped through," noted Stewart McClure, chief clerk of the Senate's education committee. "I don't think anybody had read any other title in it."

Both houses will calculate how far to go on a bill, assuming that the other body will head in the opposite direction, so they can split the difference. Seeking an immigration bill on which to campaign in 2006, House Republicans advocated a combination of securing U.S. borders against illegal immigrants and not granting amnesty to those already in the country. "Our strategy then was to pass a strong border security bill in the House, knowing the Senate would do what the Senate does and weaken it by passing a more 'comprehensive' bill," the Republican majority leader, Tom DeLay, later explained. "The subsequent conference committee would have produced a strong border security bill with some sort of limited guest worker program, something for everyone, including the president." Since the House majority can control its floor proceedings more than in the Senate, the House conferees anticipated they would be in a stronger position to dictate the terms of the final bill than their Senate counterparts. But getting a bill through the Senate required more bipartisan cooperation, and the unyielding opposition of some members to amnesty sank the bill in the Senate, a major defeat for immigration reform advocates that reverberated in the fall elections.

Serving on fewer committees, representatives often become experts in the legislation handled by those committees. In conference, they can demonstrate their knowledge of the bill, line by line. Senators, who serve on more committees, will likely have relied more on their staff to do the preliminary work on the bill and are not always vested in the compromises that shaped it, which sometimes puts them at a disadvantage in conference. The House requires all of its conferees to attend, whereas senators will attend according to their interests. A few senators, usually the chair and ranking minority members, may face a phalanx of representatives. But the senators equalize the relationship by carrying the proxy votes of their absent colleagues, and by advising the House conferees that certain provisions will never pass the Senate and will therefore kill the bill. Provisions appear and disappear in conference. Members who have shepherded a favored objective through the arduous legislative process are often frustrated to see it dropped when the conference committee tries to reconcile the larger bill's differences. Meanwhile, items that never appeared in either house's bill, or were the subject of any hearings or debate, can be inserted into the conference report.

At times the majority party may attempt to shut the minority out of conference decisions. Although the Constitution does not require that congressional business be conducted in public, the House and Senate have adopted "sunshine" reforms that require holding open committee meetings. To get around these, the conference might convene a single public session, little more than a "photo op," and then hold no other formal meetings. The majority simply needs the signatures of a majority of the conferees on the conference report. Sometimes the majority does not even invite members of the minority to participate in the conference, although this strategy, which works in the majority-rule House, can backfire in the Senate, where the minority can block passage of the conference report.

If the same party controls both the House and Senate, the joint leadership can bypass conference committees and negotiate a settlement directly between them. One house will amend the other's bill by substituting the entire language of the bill and sending it back for approval. The second house can either concur by accepting the amendment, or it can pass its own amendment and send it back. This "ping-pong" approach bounces amendments back and forth until both houses have reached an agreement on a common bill. By avoiding a conference, the majority can exclude the minority from the discussion and reduce the ability of its own mavericks to side with the minority. The amendment procedure is also used when only minor adjustments to the bill are needed, making a conference unnecessary.

Once the conference reports its compromises, each house must pass the conference version up or down, without amendments. Otherwise, the bill goes back to conference or dies.

Having survived all this, a bill can still be vetoed by the president. If Congress adjourns within ten days of sending the law to the president, the bill can simply die without the president's signature, and there is no opportunity for Congress to respond (this is known as a "pocket veto"). If Congress remains in session, however, a two-thirds vote in both chambers can override a veto. The two-thirds requirement makes vetoes hard to overturn, and just the possibility of a veto can persuade Congress to change a bill to the president's liking. Passing any bill requires agreement among "all the relevant players," House majority leader Steny Hoyer (D-Maryland) explained, "among which the president with his veto pen is a very relevant player." To forestall vetoes, Congress may pack together items the president wants and dislikes. The president must veto the entire bill, lacking the power to veto sections of a bill rather than it entirety. In 1996, Congress gave the president a "line-item veto" on appropriations to reduce federal spending, but the Supreme Court struck it down as unconstitutional. Since the Reagan administration, modern presidents have increasingly employed "signing statements" as the equivalent of a line-item veto. Presidents sign legislation as a whole while reinterpreting and attempting to modify parts to suit their purposes. The federal courts have not yet ruled on the constitutionality of such statements.

The first president to wield a veto pen forcefully was Andrew Jackson, a Democrat who vetoed twelve bills during his administration, from 1829 to 1837, most notably his veto of rechartering the Bank of the United States. The opposition Whig Party was unable to overturn any of his vetoes. Jackson viewed himself as the representative of the entire people and therefore more competent than individual members of Congress to judge the public will. His successors have frequently adopted veto strategies that pitted them against Congress. Those presidents facing opposition majorities in Congress generally view vetoes as acts of courage that show their willingness to stand firm on matters of principle. Gerald Ford (R-Michigan) had been the Republican leader in the House, but after he became president in 1974 he set himself against Congress by vetoing numerous bills to define himself as an effective executive. The Democratic majorities assisted by sending Ford bills they expected him to veto, believing that his record would defeat him in the next election.

A new president often begins an administration by signing bills that his predecessor vetoed. President Bill Clinton's first major legislative accomplishment, for instance, was the Family and Medical Leave Act of 1993, which enabled family members to take leave to attend to sick family members, after his predecessor, George H. W. Bush, had twice vetoed the bill. Members of Congress will sometimes vote for popular bills they do not favor, confident that the president will veto them. The president's party will usually vote to sustain the veto, unless the bill is more popular than the president. So, in 1972, bipartisan coalitions in Congress overrode President Richard Nixon's veto of the Clean Water Act, which he regarded as too costly but which had strong support among their constituents. Still, the veto gives the advantage to the president. Members of Congress say that their constituents will complain that they hold the majority but cannot override a veto. When they try to explain about the two-thirds requirement, they find that people outside of Congress care little about the mechanics of legislation. They just want results.

# Chapter 5
# **Checks and balances**

"When I was a Congressman I never realized how important Congress was," President John F. Kennedy once mused, "but now I do." Although Kennedy had served sixteen years in the House and Senate, it was only after he entered the White House that he appreciated the collective clout of the legislative branch, which blocked so many of his proposals.

Congress can stall a president's legislative agenda or rally behind it, most notably when new presidents come to office during a national emergency. In 1861, Abraham Lincoln and Republican majorities in Congress faced trial by Civil War, but the secession of the Southern members of Congress facilitated Republicans efforts to enact tariff, land distribution, education, and other domestic reforms that previous presidents had vetoed. In 1933, the vastly expanded Democratic majorities in the House and Senate stood ready to enact whatever Franklin D. Roosevelt sent them to get the nation out of the Depression, resulting in the rush of legislation in the "First Hundred Days" of his administration. Though President Kennedy suffered many legislative setbacks, his assassination in 1963 created an emotional climate that enabled his resourceful successor, Lyndon B. Johnson, to score dramatic legislative accomplishments in enacting his Great Society initiatives.

Legislative results rank high in measuring presidential success, a fact that has encouraged modern presidents to assume the mantle of "chief legislator" as well as chief executive. Presidents appeal to Congress to do the right thing, and apply public and offstage pressure, but ultimately they must wait for Congress to act. Treaties they negotiate must wait for approval by two-thirds of the Senate for ratification. Their appointees can take office only with the Senate's consent. The budgets they submit, recommending levels of federal spending, may be dismissed as "dead on arrival" in Congress. Presidents can veto bills, only to have Congress override those vetoes. "Congress does from a third to a half of what I think is the minimum that it ought to do," Theodore Roosevelt once commented, "and I am profoundly grateful that I get that much."

Presidents who come to office with previous experience in Congress have some advantage in dealing with the legislative branch. Even the less-than-stellar Warren G. Harding managed to forge a foreign policy in cooperation with congressional leaders, following the failure of Woodrow Wilson, for all his genius for government, to win Senate consent for the Treaty of Versailles. By contrast, Herbert Hoover, having come out of a highly successful administrative career in business and government, regarded Congress as a nuisance to be avoided as much as possible, a mind-set that contributed to his failed presidency. "He has never really recognized the House and Senate as desirable factors in our government," a political operative close to Hoover remarked. "Perhaps they are not, but that does not alter the fact that they exist and that they have equal powers."

Because strong presidents have forged links with voters, and have exerted enormous power as commander in chief, the public has come to see the presidency as the first branch of the federal government. Yet Article I spells out in detail the extensive powers of Congress, before the shorter second and third articles outline the executive and judiciary. All of this makes members of Congress sensitive of their status as an independent branch of government. "You served under eight presidents, didn't you?" a reporter once asked Speaker Sam Rayburn. "I did not serve *under* any presidents," Rayburn replied testily. "I worked *with* eight presidents."

## The chief legislator

The highlight of the president's role as chief legislator occurs with the delivery of the State of the Union address, at the start of the annual session of Congress, usually in January. On the appointed night, the vice president leads a procession of senators through the Capitol to the larger House chamber. Representatives jockey for coveted center-aisle seats, so they can be televised greeting the president's arrival and departure. Cabinet secretaries and Supreme Court justices have front-row seats reserved for them. Reporters, diplomats, family members, staff, campaign contributors, and other guests fill the galleries to capacity. None of this pomp and circumstance is required by the Constitution, which specifies simply that "from time to time" the president give Congress information on the State of the Union, and "recommend to their Consideration such Measures as he shall judge necessary and expedient" (Article II, section 3).

The first presidents, George Washington and John Adams, delivered their annual messages in person, but Thomas Jefferson regarded this practice as akin to a monarch addressing Parliament. Jefferson instead sent his messages to Congress for the clerks of the Senate and House to read aloud, and his successors followed his practice until Woodrow Wilson shattered the tradition. As a political scientist who had studied Congress, Wilson seized on the dramatic opportunities of personal appearances before a joint session to enhance the executive's legislative leadership. Over time, advances in media have expanded the audience. Calvin Coolidge's State of the Union message in 1923 was the first broadcast over radio. In 1936, Franklin D. Roosevelt persuaded Congress to shift the address from the afternoon to the evening, in prime time. Harry Truman appeared on the first televised State of the Union in 1947, and by the 1990s Bill Clinton's addresses streamed over the Internet.

For State of the Union messages, as well as for counting electoral ballots to declare a winner in the presidential election, the Senate and House are meeting in *joint session* to conduct constitutionally mandated functions. Since they are not conducting legislative business when they gather to hear a foreign head of state or other dignitaries, these are called *joint meetings*. In 1824, the

9. Clifford Berryman, longtime editorial cartoonist for the *Washington Star*, captured the feuding between Congress and the president in this cartoon that ran on July 4, 1943, with the caption: "What this country needs today is a new Declaration of INTERdependence."

Marquis de Lafayette became the first foreign guest invited to speak before Congress, and his portrait and George Washington's flank the Speaker's rostrum in the House chamber. Those who have followed him have included British prime minister Winston Churchill, Queen Elizabeth II, Israeli prime minister Menachem Begin, Russian president Boris Yeltsin, and South African president Nelson Mandela.

Nineteenth-century presidents, with Jackson and Lincoln among the few exceptions, defined their role as administrator of the laws that Congress passed and generally exercised their legislative leadership behind the scenes or through surrogates in Congress. It was Woodrow Wilson who set the precedents for making the chief executive chief legislator. Wilson admired the British parliamentary system and attempted to exert something of a prime minister's role over Congress. He worked closely with the Democratic majorities, which used rare binding-caucus rules to maintain party discipline and enact Wilson's reform legislation (in a binding caucus, party members agree to vote for whatever is decided in their caucus, a policy not repeated since then). Wilson persuaded Senate Democrats to choose a floor leader to marshal his programs, and they complied by electing the first Senate majority leader, John Worth Kern (D-Indiana). Wilson also prevailed on the Senate to adopt its first cloture rule in 1917. Following those successes, however, his presidency ended in spectacular failure. Congress was not a parliament, and Wilson remained president after his party lost its congressional majorities in 1918. During his last two years in office, he was unable to persuade the Senate to approve the Treaty of Versailles and League of Nations that he had personally negotiated.

Distrustful voters have disappointed presidents by turning control of Congresses over to the opposition party, adding an extra layer of checks and balances. Periods of divided government have produced some notable legislation, but they can also result in legislative stalemate, with the Congress ignoring the president's proposals and passing alternatives, likely to be vetoed. Notable clashes with Congress occurred during the presidencies of John Tyler (1841–45), Andrew Johnson (1865–69), and Richard Nixon (1969–74). Tyler, a former Democrat who had become a Whig, was the first vice president to assume the presidency following the death of the incumbent. He broke with the Whig Party and vetoed its key legislation. Congressional Whigs responded by rejecting most of Tyler's legislative requests and nominations. Andrew Johnson, also a former Democrat who had run on a fusion ticket with the Republican Abraham Lincoln in 1864, assumed the presidency after Lincoln's assassination. Johnson carried out what he believed were Lincoln's lenient policies in reconstructing the South after the Civil War. This put Johnson on a collision course with the Republicans who dominated Congress and were incensed over the Southern resistance to granting basic civil rights to those just freed from slavery. The constitutional clash between branches over the unprecedented problem of Reconstruction culminated in Johnson's impeachment by the House and acquittal in the Senate.

A century later, the Republican Richard Nixon faced large Democratic majorities in Congress. Seeking to circumvent Congress, Nixon impounded, or refused to spend, appropriated funds for federal programs he considered too costly and denied that he needed congressional support to pursue an unpopular war in Vietnam. Exposure of Nixon's involvement in the cover-up of the Watergate scandal, however, enabled Congress to override his vetoes of the Congressional Budget and Impoundment Act of 1974 and the War Powers Resolution, and thus restore some balance between the branches. Nixon resigned to avoid impeachment. At other times, divided government has produced bipartisan compromise. During Ronald Reagan's presidency (1981–89), when Democrats controlled the House while Republicans held the Senate for six years, Reagan got much of his program enacted by playing one house against the other.

By the twenty-first century, congressional politics grew more polarized. Faced with a trend toward party-line voting, recent presidents have concentrated on maintaining support within their own party in Congress. During George W. Bush's administration, Speaker Dennis Hastert (R-Illinois) chose not to advance bills in the House unless they had the support of "a majority of the majority"—that is, unless most House Republicans endorsed the measure—to prevent the minority from gaining the balance of power. President Barack Obama, at the start of his administration, personally visited the House Republican Conference to appeal for bipartisan support for his economic stimulus bill. When Republicans voted as a bloc against the stimulus, the president shifted tactics and negotiated between the liberal and conservative "Blue Dog" factions among congressional Democrats, to maintain majority party cohesion and enact legislation without support from the minority.

## Advice and consent

Upon entering the Oval Office, a president has thousands of appointments to make, from cabinet officers and agency heads to diplomats and federal judges. Most require confirmation by the Senate, a point of constant friction between the executive and legislature. A contributing factor to the American Revolution had been patronage abuses by royal governors, prompting most of the first state constitutions to give the appointment power to state legislatures. New York and Massachusetts, by contrast, allowed their governors to make appointments with the "advice and consent" of the legislators. After initially considered having the Senate making nominations, the framers of the Constitution adopted the "advice and consent" approach (Article II, section 2). That power went to senators on the assumption that since they represented entire states they would be better qualified than House members to judge the qualifications of nominees, particularly for the federal courts.

The right of consent carries the possibility of rejection. George Washington became the first president to feel the sting in 1789, when the Senate turned down his nomination of Benjamin Fishbourn as collector of the Port of Savannah. Although well qualified, Fishbourn lacked the support of the two senators from Georgia. This marked the first instance of "senatorial courtesy," where other senators honor the wishes of senators who oppose a nominee from their home state.

To avoid embarrassing rejections, presidents began consulting senators before submitting nominations for confirmation, which sometimes meant passing over their preferred choice for a candidate more likely to win confirmation. As a framer of the Constitution, James Madison regarded the choice of nominees to be an executive function, but as president he dropped his preferred secretary of state for a candidate the Senate wanted. Presidents who tangled with the Senate, such as John Tyler and

10. **Reflecting public interest in the event, press photographers crouched between the senators and the witness during the Senate Judiciary Committee's hearings on the 2001 nomination of former senator John Ashcroft (R-Missouri) to become attorney general.**

Andrew Johnson, suffered the indignity of having several of their cabinet and judicial nominations rejected. Tyler once submitted his nominee for secretary of the treasury three times, and each time the Senate rejected it by a larger margin.

Advice and consent powers have effectively given senators authority over who gets appointed from their states. "You appoint judges. You appoint U.S. marshals," George Smathers (D-Florida) recalled what he enjoyed most about his service in the Senate. "Any appointment that has to be confirmed you have infinitely more influence. No, being a senator is an infinitely more desirable, and influential, and powerful job than being a congressman." Once, when the American Bar Association rejected as unqualified a judicial nominee whom Senator Robert S. Kerr (D-Oklahoma) had recommended to President Kennedy, Justice Department officials sensed that Kerr took pleasure in the finding, because when the president ignored the ABA and submitted the nomination anyhow, it demonstrated Senator Kerr's legislative clout.

As a reflection of senatorial courtesy, the Senate Judiciary Committee in 1913 started the practice of "blue sheets" for all judicial branch nominations. Thereafter, each nomination had a blue sheet of paper affixed to the front of its file folder. If the blue sheet lacked the signatures of either of the home-state senators, the nomination would probably never leave the committee. The blue sheet became a mechanism to encourage consultation between the White House and the Senate. Facing this reality, presidents often selected nominees from a list of candidates submitted by the senators. As ideological battles raged over court nominations, however, adherence to the blue slip declined, and in recent years the combined opposition of both senators from a state has been required to stop a nomination.

To fill vacancies that occur during a recess of the Senate, presidents can appoint someone to hold that post until the end of the next session of Congress; they need to be approved by the Senate if they wish to serve in office any longer than that. Recess appointments enabled presidents to keep the government functioning during the many months between congressional sessions. But when Congress began meeting year round, the original purpose of recess appointments diminished. Presidents began to use it as a device to install nominees blocked in committee or in danger of rejection. Using a recess appointment in 2005, President George W. Bush named John W. Bolton as U.S. ambassador to the United Nations, over the objections of senators who regarded him as too undiplomatic for the post. Bolton held the job until he resigned in December 2006, when his recess appointment expired and it was clear that the Senate would not confirm him. When the Senate takes a brief holiday recess, presidents will announce a batch of recess appointments. President Ronald Reagan tried making recess appointments over the weekend, but the Supreme Court slapped down this practice. When the president and Senate majority come from rival parties, they usually negotiate a deal by which the president agrees not to make recess appointments in return for a pledge to allow some of the more controversial nominations to reach a vote. President George W. Bush refused to commit to such an agreement, and the Senate resorted to holding pro forma sessions, in which one senator gaveled the Senate open and closed in a few seconds, every few days, to avoid technically going into recess.

Allen Drury's best-selling novel and motion picture *Advise and Consent* centered on the rejection of a controversial choice for secretary of state. The Senate has actually confirmed 95 percent of all cabinet nominations, but it has rejected a third of all those nominated to the Supreme Court. Senators reason that presidents deserve advisors who agree with them and in whom they can trust, and that executive branch appointments will not extend beyond the president's term. The judiciary, by contrast, is an independent branch whose members hold office for life, pending good behavior.

Judicial nominations have grown exceedingly contentious. In the nineteenth century, Supreme Court nominations went directly to the Senate floor, rather than to committee. Senators debated these nominations behind closed doors to shield the nominees' privacy and to talk candidly (although their discussion and vote invariably leaked to the press). By the twentieth century, the Judiciary Committee held hearings and called nominees to testify in their own behalf and answer the senators' questions. Administration "handlers" now accompany the nominees and advise them to show due deference to the senators rather than debate them. Judicial nominees must try to appear open to questions while at the same time not revealing how they might rule on matters of consequence.

Because of their lifetime appointments, federal court nominations have long stirred political passions. The Senate rejected a Supreme Court nomination as early as 1795. There was intense conservative opposition to the nominations of Louis Brandeis in 1916 and Felix Frankfurter in 1939; they both went on to distinguish themselves on the bench. In 1968 conservatives filibustered against Lyndon Johnson's nomination of the liberal Abe Fortas to be chief justice, and in 1969 and 1970 liberals rejected two of Richard Nixon's conservative appointments to the Supreme Court, Clement Haynsworth, for questionable finances, and G. Harrold Carswell, for questionable competency.

In 1987, President Reagan's nomination of the conservative former solicitor general Robert Bork to the Supreme Court set off a fierce confrontation in the Senate. No one questioned Bork's legal abilities, but his strong opinions and ideological leanings raised objections. Bork verbally sparred with senators at his hearing, largely talking himself out of the job. His opponents ran a national advertising campaign against his nomination and lobbied senators to vote against him. Ever since his defeat, nominees subject to such organized campaigns have been said to be "borked."

A White House congressional liaison, Tom Korologos, who assisted hundreds of nominees, including Judge Bork, in navigating their confirmation hearings, advised them to accept the fact that the hearings will not be fair: "You have no rights, there is no provision for 'objecting.' Hearsay questions are allowed. A U.S. senator can ask any question he or she chooses. So be polite and deferential . . . . The goal is to demonstrate your qualifications while getting out unscathed."

The nomination of a federal judge follows a complex process. The president announces the appointment, the FBI investigates the nominee's background, and the American Bar Association evaluates the nominee's judicial qualifications. The nominee will need to complete lengthy questionnaires from both the Justice Department and the Senate Judiciary Committee. Months may go by between the announcement and the nomination's arrival at the committee. The nominee will be invited to testify at a hearing and later given time to respond to any questions that might have been raised. The committee will then vote to report the nomination to the full Senate, which might reject or confirm the nominee. If there is significant opposition, the committee may bottle the nomination up and never report it out, in which case the president might withdraw the name rather than face defeat. The committee can reject the nomination or report it out with a negative vote. On the floor, senators can place holds on the nomination or filibuster against it. Faced with such delaying tactics against a number of his judicial nominations, George W. Bush demanded "up-or-down" votes on his nominations, claiming that it was unconstitutional to require more than a majority vote to confirm. But the Constitution allows the Senate to write its own rules (Article I, section 5).

## War and peace

"By and large, the Congress is not much help to a president in matters of foreign policy," former undersecretary of state Nicholas Katzenbach concluded, because of the lack of "political profit" in it. Yet his own experiences in dealing with the Vietnam War taught Katzenbach that the president alone "simply cannot hold the overwhelming public support he needs for any length of time without the strong support of Congress." Sharing power in foreign policy was therefore not so much a constitutional question as a "practical political one." Presidential defenders reason that there cannot be 535 secretaries of state or commanders in chief. Presidents generally take the lead in matters of war and peace and regard congressional involvement in foreign policy as intrusive, despite Congress' constitutional power to regulate foreign commerce, confirm diplomatic appointments, approve treaties, and declare war. Unlike the executive, the legislature does not speak with a single voice. The people's representatives reflect public opinion, which is often divided on America's involvement abroad.

The Constitution gives the president the "Power, by and with the Advice and Consent of the Senate, to make Treaties provided two thirds of the Senators present concur" (Article II, section 2). The meaning of "consent" is clear, but "advice" is murky. Members of Congress complain that presidents rarely ask their advice in advance of a treaty that reshapes public policy and too often prefer to inform them just before announcing it publicly. They talk of wanting to be there for the take-off instead of the crash landing.

In the First Congress, senators wanted President Washington to come to their chamber when making nominations and requesting that treaties be ratified, to seek their advice as well as their consent. Washington demurred, reasoning that the abundance of nominations would make this impractical. He would send nominations to the Senate but agreed to the protocol of carrying treaties to their chamber in person. He did this on August 22, 1789, placing before the Senate a list of questions about treaties with Southern Indian tribes (which were at that time treated as separate nations). Washington's imposing figure made it awkward to debate in his presence, and the noise of the street traffic from below made it hard to hear the questions being read. So the senators referred the matter to a committee. "This defeats every purpose of my coming here," Washington protested, storming out of the chamber. He cooled down sufficiently to return to receive the Senate's suggestions, but after that incident he never went back. Most other presidents have kept their distance and sent treaties to the Senate by messenger, although Woodrow Wilson personally went to the Capitol to appeal for approval of the Versailles Treaty and U.S. membership in the League of Nations, which the Senate twice rejected.

Congress formally declared war against Great Britain in 1812, against Mexico in 1846, against Spain in 1898, against Germany and Austria-Hungary in 1917, and against Japan and Germany in 1941. On other occasions, the president has acted independently as commander in chief. In 1801, when Barbary pirates in the Mediterranean harassed American shipping, President Thomas Jefferson sidestepped legislators by instructing the navy to enforce existing treaties with North Africa and "chastise" the pirates by destroying their ships, a police action short of war. In 1950, when Communist North Korea invaded South Korea, the United Nations Security Council called on member nations to repel the aggressors. Congress was in recess at the time, but President Harry Truman believed that he could unilaterally endorse the UN resolution and dispatch American combat troops on his authority as commander in chief, rather than wait for a congressional declaration of war. Congress returned to enact appropriations to pay for this military action, but Senator Robert A. Taft warned senators that by accepting Truman's usurpation of congressional war power they faced its permanent loss. When public opinion later turned against the war, Truman rather than Congress bore the brunt of public displeasure. Nevertheless, Truman had established a precedent, and no president has formally sought a declaration of war since World War II.

Using its power of the purse, Congress can restrain military action by cutting off funds, although this exposes members to the politically risky charge of abandoning American troops in combat. Though it is often asserted that Congress ended the Vietnam War by cutting off funds, the story was more complicated. In 1969, after five years of combat and twenty-five thousand American deaths, an amendment to the Defense Appropriations Act barred U.S. ground combat activity from spreading into Laos or Thailand. In 1970, the Cooper-Church Amendment aimed at prohibiting President Richard Nixon from using funds for military action in Cambodia, although it did not become law until after U.S. troops had left Cambodia. Between 1971 and 1973, Congress debated several other amendments to cut off funds and withdraw all U.S. troops from Southeast Asia, but adopted none of them. Not until June 1973, following the peace agreement and withdrawal of U.S. combat troops, did Congress bar funding any further military operations. In 1974, the Foreign Assistance Act set a ceiling of four thousand civilian and military personnel in Vietnam, to be cut to three thousand within a year. In 1975, Congress rejected President Gerald Ford's request for emergency funds to support the South Vietnamese government, which soon fell to the North Vietnamese.

Congress attached to the 1974 Trade Act the Jackson-Vanik Amendment, sponsored by Senator Henry Jackson (D-Washington) and Representative Charles Vanik (D-Ohio). The amendment denied normal trade relations to nations that restricted emigration, arguing that this was a violation of basic human rights, and was aimed at allowing Jewish dissenters to leave the Soviet Union. Although the amendment ran contrary to the Ford administration's efforts to reach detente with the Soviets, President Ford recognized the overwhelming support for the measure in Congress and signed it. The Soviet Union protested but eventually complied, and the amendment ultimately enabled a million Russians to immigrate to Israel and a half million to the United States.

In 1982 the Boland amendment to a defense appropriations bill, sponsored by Representative Edward Boland (D-Massachusetts), prohibited the Reagan administration from funding anti-Communist Contra rebels in Nicaragua. This led to the Iran-Contra investigation when the administration was caught evading the law by funneling money from arms sales in the Middle East to the Contras in Central America. In 1993, Congress cut off funds for further military operations in Somalia, and in 1994 it prohibited U.S. military action in Rwanda. But after the United States became bogged down militarily in Iraq, Congress failed in its efforts to cut funds or set a timetable for military withdrawal. Even when public sentiment turns against a war, the most feasible option for resolving that conflict is usually for Congress to conduct a public debate that will bring pressure on the administration for peace.

Congress rallied behind the president after the terrorist attacks on September 11, 2001, when it passed a resolution authorizing George W. Bush "to use all necessary and appropriate force against those nations, organizations or persons" who planned or committed the assault. The next year, President Bush won congressional support for a preventive war to overthrow the regime of Saddam Hussein in Iraq. The congressional resolution authorized the use of force against Iraq in a manner "necessary and appropriate" to protect U.S. national security and enforce United Nations resolutions, encouraging the president to pursue diplomatic solutions before launching an attack. Among the critics, Senator Robert C. Byrd (D-West Virginia) accused Congress of "handing the president unchecked authority." But the House of Representatives voted 296 to 133 and the Senate 77 to 23 for the resolution, with many members feeling unable to oppose a president on a matter of national security just a month before the congressional elections.

Dismayed by the executive branch's failure to keep Congress informed, Senator Arlen Specter predicted that future historians would look back on the years immediately following 9/11 as "an era of unbridled executive power and congressional ineffectiveness." American historians and political scientists for years had defended presidential prerogatives and regarded the Congress as a drag on foreign policy, but they came to rethink those assumptions. During the Vietnam War, the historian Arthur Schlesinger Jr. concluded that their "delight in a strong presidency" had been based on agreement with the policies that strong presidents pursued. When confronted with presidential policies that seemed headed for disaster, scholars began to reevaluate the congressional role. But Schlesinger acknowledged that it would be hard for Congress to restrain a presidential drive toward enlargement of a war, since "voting against military appropriations is both humanly and politically self-defeating."

## Congress investigates

The most potent weapon in the congressional arsenal against an "imperial presidency" is its power to investigate wrongdoing in matters of foreign, military, or domestic policy. In *McGrain v. Daughtery* (1927), the Supreme Court confirmed the right of congressional committees to subpoena anyone inside or outside the government; in *Sinclair v. United States* (1929) it declared that congressional investigations need not be tied to pending legislation but can deal with anything necessary to understand the effect of laws already passed. However, after the excesses of the anti-Communist investigations in the 1940s and '50s, the court added the caveat, in *Watkins v. United States* (1957), that witnesses retained their constitutional protections under the Bill of Rights (including the right not to incriminate themselves) when they testified before Congress.

Congress held its first investigation in 1792, after American Indians defeated a military expedition commanded by General Arthur St. Clair, killing six hundred U.S. troops. A select committee of the House of Representatives called witnesses and examined government records. In the first instance of a president invoking "executive privilege," George Washington stipulated that the committee could view records only at the War Department.

The committee eventually exonerated General St. Clair, blaming the War Department for having inadequately supplied his troops. During the Civil War, Congress investigated ineptitude in the Union Army and tried to direct the military policies of the Lincoln administration, including the appointment of army generals. After the war, Congress investigated a number of scandals, most notably Credit Mobilier in 1872, which exposed that two vice presidents and several members of Congress had accepted stock in a railroad being built with federal subsidies.

Early in the twentieth century, the construction of vast caucus rooms in the Senate and House office buildings provided the setting for some dramatic congressional investigations. These imposing marble rooms gave the hearings the appearance of grand opera: magnificent settings, enormous casts, and convoluted plots, with everyone waiting for the witnesses to sing. Investigations epitomized the American system of separation of powers, in which the independent legislature could scrutinize issues that the executive would prefer to remain hidden and uncover wrongdoing at all levels of government.

Investigations can lead to exposure and punishment of malfeasance. The press had reacted skeptically when the Senate looked into some questionable leasing of federal oil reserves at Teapot Dome, Wyoming, in 1923. Reporters had seen too many congressional investigations begin with a fanfare of press releases before fading away inconclusively. But the committee's chairman, Thomas Walsh (D-Montana), persistently interrogated witnesses until they implicated President Warren Harding's secretary of the interior, Albert Fall, in a bribery scheme. Fall became the first cabinet member to go to prison.

Investigations can trigger legislative responses. After the stock market crashed in 1929 and the nation plunged into the Great Depression, the Senate Banking Committee held a highly publicized investigation of Wall Street banking and brokerage practices that led to the New Deal's landmark banking and securities regulation legislation.

Investigations can also shape political careers. The diligent investigation of national defense production during World War II by Senator Harry S. Truman (D-Missouri) led to his nomination for vice president in 1944. In 1951, the televised congressional investigations into organized crime in the United States made its chairman, Senator Estes Kefauver (D-Tennessee), a presidential contender. But the raucous hearings of the House Committee on Un-American Activities, and the Senate Permanent Subcommittee on Investigations chaired by Senator Joseph R. McCarthy (R-Wisconsin), into the threat of Communist subversion and espionage, raised concerns about the investigators' infringement of civil liberties. McCarthy's bullying tactics destroyed reputations without proving his charges. His freewheeling investigations came to an end when his own committee investigated charges and countercharges between McCarthy and the U.S. Army. Following the Army-McCarthy hearings in 1954, a broad bipartisan majority of the Senate censured McCarthy for conduct unbecoming a senator.

During the Vietnam War, in 1966, Senate Foreign Relations Committee chairman J. William Fulbright (D-Arkansas) conducted "educational" hearings into the conduct of the war. By calling prominent opponents of the war to testify along with administration defenders, Fulbright heightened public awareness of the antiwar movement. The most famous congressional investigation looked into the burglary of the Democratic National Committee headquarters at the Watergate building during the presidential election of 1972. Chaired by Senator Sam Ervin (D-North Carolina), the committee uncovered copious evidence that the Nixon administration used "dirty tricks" against its political opponents. The televised hearings drew a large national audience who watched as senators grilled administration witnesses and discovered that the president had been secretly tape-recording his conversations. After the Supreme Court rejected President Nixon's claim of executive privilege in withholding these tapes, their release implicated him in a cover-up. He resigned rather than face certain impeachment.

By contrast, the joint Iran-Contra investigation in 1987 produced less conclusive results. The committee had to grant limited immunity to gain testimony from several key witnesses, but this immunity later caused the Supreme Court to overturn their convictions. In 1996, a select committee of the Senate investigated President Bill Clinton's investment in a failed real estate development called Whitewater, holding sixty days of public hearings and calling 136 witnesses to testify. Republicans and Democrats on the committee filed completely contradictory reports, and the hearings had no impact on Clinton's reelection. Clinton, who lost money on the investment, later jested that Congress had spent seven million dollars trying to prove that he was corrupt *and* stupid. Reacting to this anticlimax, one journalist suggested that Congress ought to investigate why it had to investigate everything.

Yet, congressional investigations and oversight of government agencies have served as a significant check on the executive branch. They reflect James Madison's dictum that the great difficulty in framing a government is: "You must first enable the government to control the governed; and in the next place, oblige it to control itself." Investigations provide the means for government self-control by aiming the spotlight of publicity on wrongdoing and producing legislative solutions. As the Watergate inquiry demonstrated, a successful investigation requires investigators to collect and sort through the evidence, and to apply some shrewdness to evaluating evidence and questioning witnesses. They must show a willingness to treat witnesses seriously and with some degree of humanity, make some meaningful effort to rise above partisanship, and demonstrate some showmanship in holding press and public attention. Ultimately, the success of a congressional investigation is measured by the determination of Congress to take what it learned to prevent the uncovered problems from occurring again.

## Punishment and protection

The ultimate punishment of official misconduct is the impeachment of federal officials, anyone from judges to cabinet officers and the president. Just the threat of impeachment has been enough to convince a recalcitrant agency head to release documents being held back from Congress or to resign from office. But impeachment is a drastic and arduous process that can inflict as much damage on its sponsors as its intended target.

The equivalent of an indictment, impeachment requires a majority vote in the House. Officials can be impeached for "high crimes and misdemeanors," a phrase that is sufficiently vague to cover a multitude of sins. The Senate will hold a trial to hear evidence, but it takes a two-thirds vote of the senators to convict and remove that person from office. The requirement of a supermajority in the Senate has served as a brake on the use of impeachment for political purposes: A partisan vote in the House is unlikely to produce a bipartisan conviction in the Senate.

When Jeffersonian Republicans won the election of 1800, they ousted the Federalists from control of the White House and Congress, but the courts remained packed with Federalist judges. Rather than wait for their retirement, the Jeffersonians in the House pursued impeachment proceedings against the most obstreperous judges. The Senate's failure to convict and remove Supreme Court Justice Samuel Chase in 1804, however, set a precedent against impeaching judges for their political views. During the struggle between congressional Republicans and President Andrew Johnson over the reconstruction of the South, the House in 1868 impeached Johnson. Since Republicans held more than a two-thirds majority in the Senate, his conviction seemed likely, but fear of weakening the presidency convinced seven Republican senators to defect. Johnson won acquittal by a single vote. After the Senate's investigation of the Watergate scandal, the House Judiciary Committee in 1974 began voting on articles of impeachment against President Richard Nixon. With his support in Congress eroding, Nixon chose to resign rather than stand trial in the Senate.

During the 1980s, the House impeached three federal judges on charges of perjury, corruption, and tax fraud. Rather than hear the testimony as a body, senators streamlined the proceedings by appointing a special committee to weigh the evidence first and then report back. The full Senate then cast the final vote, and each of the judges was convicted by lopsided margins. One of them, Walter Nixon, sued on the grounds that the committee process was unconstitutional. However, in *Nixon v. United States* (1993) the Supreme Court found that the Senate had the sole power under the Constitution to conduct a trial and could do so as it saw fit.

In 1998, House Republicans moved to impeach President Bill Clinton for having perjured himself by denying an affair with a White House intern. For a presidential impeachment trial, the chief justice presides (since the vice president, as president of the Senate, would succeed to the presidency after a conviction). In this presidential trial, the Senate as a whole heard the evidence, rather than delegate that job to a committee. The House vote against Clinton largely followed party lines, which made it unlikely that the House managers could achieve the needed two-thirds vote for conviction in the Senate. Clinton was acquitted and finished his term as president. The collapse of the Clinton impeachment reinforced congressional wariness about using impeachment as a political device. Opinion polls showed that the public regarded the president's impeachment as an overzealous effort and that his removal from office would be excessive, despite his deplorable conduct.

Just as Congress investigates presidents, the Department of Justice pursues wrongdoing among members of Congress. In the 1980 "Abscam" scandal, agents of the Federal Bureau of Investigation posed as Arab sheiks offering money to a few members of Congress in return for their promise to introduce private immigration bills. The transactions were videotaped and led to the prosecution and conviction of a senator and five representatives.

In their ongoing adversary relationship, however, members of the legislative branch enjoy the protection of the Constitution's "speech or debate" clause (Article 1, section 6). Dating back to the struggles between the British parliament and the king, this provision specifies that to prevent the executive from interfering with legitimate legislative activity, members of Congress cannot be prosecuted for what they say in debate or be arrested while on their way to attend a session of Congress. But federal prosecutors complain that this provision has shielded members from criminal investigations. In 2006, FBI agents raided the Capitol Hill office of Representative William Jefferson (D-Louisiana) and seized documents to document charges of bribery and corruption against him. Jefferson claimed that the raid on his office violated his speech or debate privilege, and the Republican Speaker of the House sided with him against the Department of Justice. In *U.S. v. Rayburn House Office Building, Room 2113* (2007), the federal courts allowed government prosecutors to use only some of the evidence it collected, imposing limits to make sure that all legislative material had been filtered out. In 2008, when Representative Rick Renzi (R-Arizona) called on the courts to throw out charges of fraud and extortion because federal agents wiretapped his conversations with other members of Congress, the leadership of both parties in the House backed Renzi's position. These cases raised questions about what constitutes "legislative activity." Congressional leaders worry that if the courts weaken these protections, a president might someday use the precedent for political retribution.

Despite their constitutional protection, some members of Congress have been convicted of crimes. Matthew Lyon was serving as a U.S. representative from Vermont in 1798 when he was convicted under the Alien and Sedition Acts for having published articles critical of the government in his newspaper. While he was still serving his four months in jail, he won reelection to another term. Once in office, members accused of infractions of House and Senate rules can be censured by majority vote. Those convicted of serious crimes can be expelled, by a two-thirds vote. Most of those facing expulsion have chosen to resign before a formal vote was taken.

## Congress and the courts

The judiciary plays the arbiter in disputes between the executive and legislative branches, holding the power to rule acts of Congress and actions of the president unconstitutional and illegal. Although Congress's relationship with the federal courts has not been as contentious as that with the president, the courts have periodically ruffled legislative feathers by exercising judicial review. In the case of *Marbury v. Madison* (1803) the Supreme Court first claimed the right to declare acts of Congress unconstitutional, an implied rather than explicit right in the Constitution. The opinion written by Chief Justice John Marshall struck down a portion of the Judiciary Act.

Members of Congress express outrage when the courts undo their handiwork, complaining of "judicial activism," a process by which unelected judges make law through their rulings. When the courts throw out a law, Congress can respond by rewriting it to address judicial concerns, strip the court of jurisdiction over the matter, or propose a constitutional amendment to reverse the decision—as it did with the Sixteenth Amendment, after the Supreme Court rejected the income tax as unconstitutional. The Supreme Court's most controversial decisions, from banning prayer in public schools to supporting a woman's right to an abortion, have prompted members of Congress to introduce constitutional amendments. Yet of the more than ten thousand formally proposed over the past two centuries, only thirty-three amendments have been passed by Congress and only twenty-seven were ratified by the states. The Constitution has been amended only when a broad national consensus on an issue existed.

With judicial review in mind, Congress drafts committee reports to outline what it intended when it passed a law. Courts will then consider the entire legislative history, committee reports and hearings, along with the floor debates, as a guide in interpreting the law. Some judges prefer to consider the text of the statute alone rather than trying to divine the intent of the legislators. In the case of *Edwards v. Agullard* (1987), Justice Antonin Scalia punctured the notion of courts determining legislative intent by listing some of the factors that may have determined a legislator's vote: "He may have thought the bill would provide jobs for his district, or may have wanted to make amends with a faction of the party he had alienated on another close vote, or he may have been a close friend of the bill's sponsor, or he may have been repaying a favor owned the Majority leader ... or he may have been pressured to vote for a bill he disliked by a wealthy contributor or by a flood of constituent mail, or he may have been reluctant to hurt the feelings of a loyal staff member who worked on the bill, or he may have been settling an old score with a legislator who opposed the bill, or he may have been intoxicated and utterly unmotivated when the vote was called, or he may have accidentally voted 'yes' instead of 'no,' or, of course, he may have had (and very likely did have) a combination of some of the above motives."

The courts usually keep hands off the internal business of Congress, noting that the Constitution allows each house to run itself (Article I, section 5). Federal judges have, for instance, dismissed citizens' suits against the hiring of congressional chaplains because of its violation of the separation of church and state, on the grounds that the Constitution allows the Senate and House to elect their own officers, and the chaplains are elected officers. In an exception, *Wesberry v. Sanders* (1964), the Supreme Court required that all House districts be roughly equal in population, ending a system that had privileged smaller rural districts over larger urban ones. The ruling gave more representatives to urban and suburban districts, which fostered issues that their constituencies favored, such as environmentalism.

Court rulings influence the legislative process because members of Congress must weigh provisions of a bill that might not pass judicial review, as well as adjust the legislation in response to an unfavorable decision. Courts also shape the way executive agencies interpret and administer the laws, and intervene in confrontations between the president and Congress, such as defining what a president can withhold from Congress under "executive privilege."

The courts have given Congress wide latitude in defining its constitutional powers, particularly in the use of the commerce clause, regulating interstate commerce, to set minimum wages and maximum hours of work, establish public health policies, and promote racial integration and civil rights. The courts have also agreed that Congress can delegate some of its powers to independent regulatory commissions, although not to the executive branch. The Supreme Court struck down the New Deal's National Recovery Administration (NRA) in *Schechter Poultry Corp. v. United States* (1935), known as the "sick chicken" case because the NRA had authorized trade organizations to regulate the quality of chickens being sold. The court concluded that Congress could neither delegate its powers to nongovernment trade groups nor regulate as interstate commerce items produced and consumed within the same state. The Supreme Court also struck down the "legislative veto," in *Immigration and Naturalization Service v. Chadha* (1983), a device that permitted the administration to set certain regulations unless rejected by either the House or Senate. The high court found the procedure unconstitutional because it allowed improper delegation of legislative power to the executive branch, and because allowing a single house to veto a provision violated the principles of bicameralism.

The constant struggle between Congress, the president, and the courts acts out Madison's dictum that the ambition of each branch be set to counteract the others. Each has guarded its own prerogatives, while trying to poach on the others. Although messy, the arrangement of checks and balances has preserved the original structure of government while allowing it to grow to meet the vastly expanded demands of the modern nation.

# Chapter 6
## The Capitol complex

Awed by the soaring dome, marble pillars, and statue-lined corridors, sightseers may perceive the U.S. Capitol as a combination art gallery and historical museum, not appreciating that its prime function is to house the Congress. To accommodate an extended community of senators, representatives, staff, journalists, lobbyists, and curious visitors, the Capitol complex has steadily expanded into a multitude of office buildings linked by tunnels. Outside on the lawns, Civil War soldiers have drilled, demonstrators have protested, and inaugural spectators have thronged. Inside, the Capitol sometimes has taken on the air of a county fair. Church services, funerals, auctions, and theatrical performances have taken place there, and hawkers peddled fruit, cigars, candy, pies, sandwiches, and souvenirs from its corridors until 1890 when Speaker Thomas B. Reed (R-Maine) banned vendors from their niches in Statuary Hall. Decades later the Capitol could still be described as a "city within a building," a complex containing restaurants, banks, barber shops, gymnasiums, libraries, post offices, subway lines, and its own power plant.

The Senate and House are situated on Capitol Hill much the same way a liberal arts college coexists with an engineering school on the same campus; they occupy nearby space but otherwise have little to do with each other. A star on the floor in the center of the

**11. The Capitol is the most identifiable symbol of American democracy.**

rotunda marks the dividing point between the two. The House and Senate each control their respective halves of the Capitol, and even longtime occupants sometimes have trouble finding their way on the other side. Indeed, resentment of the "other body" surfaces at times, such as during the presidential impeachment trial in 1999, when the House managers grumbled about having to ascend to "Mount Olympus."

# The Capitol

When Pierre L'Enfant mapped the future national capital in 1791,
he identified the high ground known as Jenkins Hill as a "pedestal
waiting for a monument." Renamed Capitol Hill in an effort to graft
the fledgling republic onto Roman roots, it became the site of the
U.S. Capitol Building, whose imposing dome stands as a symbol of
American democracy. A veteran House member urged newcomers
to look up at the dome whenever they headed to the chamber to
vote. "If you reach a point when it doesn't give you goose bumps," he
advised, "draft your resignation letter the next day."

The Capitol's familiar appearance has actually evolved over
time, growing along with the nation. When Congress arrived in
Washington in 1800, only the boxlike Senate wing of the building
stood completed, and into it crowded the Senate, the House of
Representatives, the Supreme Court, and the Library of Congress.
The House wing was ready in 1807, connected to the Senate wing by
a wooden walkway before the rotunda was completed. Congress was
out of session when the British invaded in August 1814 and torched
the Capitol. A summer storm saved the exterior walls, but the
intense fire destroyed most of the interior. All that survived within
the original building was a vestibule containing a set of "corncob
columns," classic Roman columns that the architect Benjamin Henry
Latrobe had Americanized by adding corncobs for decoration.

Rebuilt in the 1820s, the Capitol was topped by a low dome,
modeled after Rome's Parthenon. Over the next thirty years, the
influx of legislators from the new western states filled the building
beyond capacity, and new wings were ordered constructed to
house vastly larger chambers. The new construction put the old
dome out of proportion, so an immense cast-iron dome replaced
it. Part sandstone, part marble, part cast iron painted white, the
building echoes the motto on the Great Seal of the United States:
*E Pluribus Unum*—out of many, one.

Construction of the Capitol relied on local slave labor, hired out by their owners. Slavery existed in the District of Columbia until Congress abolished it there in 1862. The bronze statute of Freedom that stands above the dome was cast by Philip Reid, an enslaved man who had been freed by the time it was installed atop the Capitol in 1863. Immigrant stonemasons and artisans also contributed to the building. These Old World artists decorated its interiors with New World images. They were fascinated with Native Americans, who frequently appear in the Capitol's artwork, but slavery was too contentious to depict. No African American appeared in the Capitol's art until the painter Emmanuel Leutze added a black pioneer to his massive mural, *Westward the Course of Empire Takes Its Way*, soon after Lincoln signed the first Emancipation Proclamation in 1862.

In the years after the Civil War, the landscape architect Frederick Law Olmsted added formal landscaping for the Capitol grounds and constructed terraces that gave the Capitol's West Front a more formal appearance (where they now serve as the presidential inaugural platform). Standing on the East Front plaza today, almost every building in sight represents some function of the government that was housed in the original Capitol, including the Supreme Court and Library of Congress. The burning of the Capitol in 1814 destroyed the congressional library as well. Congress purchased former President Thomas Jefferson's personal library as a replacement, and his eclectic interests ensured that Congress would have more than a law library. The Congressional Library occupied three floors across the West Front of the Capitol, halfway between the House and Senate. Its wooden shelving led to some spectacular blazes, even without the help of the British. The fireproof cast-iron shelves that were installed in the 1850s inspired the use of cast iron in building the new dome, which was triple the size of the original. The lighter material enabled the larger dome to rest on the existing walls.

The exterior of the Capitol resembles a Roman temple, while its bright interior frescoes suggest an Italian church, thanks to the nineteenth-century Italian painter Constantino Brumidi. A political exile, Brumidi brought to the Capitol in 1855 a style of fresco painting he had learned at the Vatican. The military engineer in charge of expanding the Capitol, Montgomery C. Meigs, had been skeptical at first but became transfixed by Brumidi's deft illustrations and vivid colors, which would be preserved when the plaster and paint dried. Brumidi received contracts to paint the canopy high above the rotunda and also many committee rooms and halls. He worked mostly on the Senate side, since the House regarded ceiling painting as undemocratic. The House relented in the 1970s, when the artist Allyn Cox decorated its halls with scenes from American history.

Less ornate, the House and Senate chambers are stately rooms where members debate and vote, mingle and converse. Often there are just a few members in attendance, but whenever votes are held, members flock to the chambers and enjoy a rare opportunity in their crowded schedules to stop and talk with each other—over the din. These informal interludes have been compared to "a cocktail party without cocktails." Clustering about, sharing news and swapping stories, they measure each other's interests and personalities, cut deals, and plan tactics.

The House and Senate have each occupied several chambers within the Capitol. In 1800 the Senate met in a large room on the ground floor of the Senate wing, while the House was squeezed into a set of rooms that would eventually be occupied by a single Senate leader. A bronze plaque outside that door commemorates the first order of business when the House occupied the rooms: they had to decide the presidential election between Thomas Jefferson and Aaron Burr, who had tied in the Electoral College. The House moved in 1807 to its own chamber, a handsome room currently known as Statuary Hall, which at its opening constituted the largest public space in the United States. The House met there until 1857, and during those years its membership grew from 142 to 237. Meanwhile, the Senate wing was remodeled and the Senate moved upstairs to a new chamber on the second floor, with the Supreme Court taking over the original space on the ground floor.

Thirty-four senators first occupied the Old Senate Chamber in 1810, and that number had doubled by the time the Senate vacated the room in 1859. In January of that year, senators moved into the current chamber. The future leaders of the Union and Confederacy walked together in that procession, which included Jefferson Davis, both of Abraham Lincoln's vice presidents, and members of the cabinets and military ranks on opposite sides during the Civil War. Leading the procession was Vice President John C. Breckinridge, a cousin of Mary Todd Lincoln. He would later become a Confederate officer and lead an 1864 raid on Washington. Breckinridge and his Confederate troops got close enough to see the Capitol's completed dome before being driven back by federal forces.

Poor acoustics in the House chamber made it hard to hear speakers—many fine orators entered, members lamented, never to be heard from again. By contrast, the Old Senate Chamber's theater-perfect acoustics facilitated the Senate's "Golden Age of Debate" in the three decades preceding the Civil War, when Webster, Clay, and Calhoun held forth. Audio in the new, larger Senate chamber was never as clear, however, and the quality of debate suffered for it. A glass ceiling let in light but absorbed sound. Reporters of debate had to sprint back and forth across the chamber in order to hear both sides of a debate. Replacement of the glass with a plaster ceiling in 1950 did not noticeably improve the acoustics, and microphones were finally installed in 1971 so the senators could be heard. The House chamber was similarly remodeled, and members use microphones while speaking at podiums in the well, the lower floor at the front of the hall.

Neither chamber allows visitors to lean on the balconies, a prohibition dating back to December 1916, when woman suffrage activists interrupted Woodrow Wilson's State of the Union message by draping a banner over the balcony in the House chamber: "Mr. President, What Will You Do for Woman Suffrage?" Other demonstrators have also used the Capitol as a symbolic backdrop. Environmentalists once dumped a ton of coal on the Capitol grounds; farmers set sheep loose on the lawn; and a group seeking to protect endangered wildlife brought a cheetah to a congressional hearing. Congress dabbles in the symbolic as well. After passing legislation to repeal the marriage tax penalty, Republicans had a bride and groom carry the bill to the White House, and Democrats later sent one of their energy bills to the president in a fuel-efficient hybrid car.

The Senate and House galleries are open to visitors, and technology has expanded the audience nationally and internationally. Radio began broadcasting from the Capitol in 1923, and television arrived in 1947. The floor proceedings remained off limits, however, until the House permitted televising them in 1979 and the Senate in 1986. Some members have regretted ever permitting the TV cameras in, blaming television for heightening partisanship and confrontation, since members now felt they had to speak on every issue and answer every charge.

At first, anyone could wander onto the floor before the House and Senate had convened that day. A senator once complained that he had to elbow his way through a crowd of people to get to his desk, and then found someone already sitting there. Although loath to do anything that might offend constituents, senators finally banned visitors, except for journalists. Reporters were permitted on the Senate floor just before a day's session to get a briefing from the leadership on the day's schedule (in the House, similar briefings were held in the Speaker's offices). Known as "dugout chatter" from the term for a baseball pre-game broadcast, this privilege was also suspended, until even staff needed special permission to get access to the floor. The only other way to get there is by election.

## The members

Capitol Hill is divided between members of Congress and everyone else. Signs on elevators and restrooms proclaim Members Only and Senators Only. Dining rooms and parking spaces are reserved for the members. The institution is designed to help the elected to do their jobs. After each election, Capitol police, elevator operators, and other staff receive photo crib sheets to help them identify new members, and all go out of their way to assist them. A freshman representative, on his way to the Capitol to cast a vote, waited on the curb for the red light to turn, not realizing that the police were holding the traffic for the members during the vote. "It's green for you," the officer explained.

Congress reflects the nation, although not as an exact mirror. Its membership has always contained a disproportionate number of lawyers and business executives, although it has also attracted doctors, ministers, military and police officers, journalists, athletes, farmers, and some blue-collar workers. For much of its history, Congress was predominantly white and male. Women and minorities have increased their ranks in the House and Senate but remain below their national proportions. Religious affiliation has become more diverse, with Protestants still the most numerous group but diminishing compared with the growing ranks of Catholics and Jews. The first Muslim was elected to the House in 2007 and the first Buddhist in 2008. The majority of members held previous political office before coming to Congress. House members often served in state or local office, and half the senators previously served in the House. The congressional staff has also become a springboard, with an increasing number of staff members running for seats vacated by their bosses.

The Constitution originally set the first Monday in December for the beginning of a new Congress, thirteen months after the elections (Article I, section 4). In those days, the average session would run from December through to spring. In 1933, the Twentieth Amendment moved the opening date forward to January 3, but even then Congress continued to meet for only half the year. Members would bring their families to Washington and after adjournment would pack up to return home for the rest of the year. Their children would go back to their local schools, and the members would resume their law practices and other business ventures. As Congress stretched to year-long sessions, stricter ethics rules restricted what work members could do outside of their official duties. Members with young families urged the leadership to announce vacation schedules well in advance, and in 1971 Congress passed a law providing for an annual recess during the month of August (which could be suspended when extra time was needed for legislative business). The House and Senate leadership planned recesses around national holidays and religious observances, allowing members to spend that time with their families and constituents. They may also go abroad on congressional delegations, known as CODELs. These fact-finding trips acquaint members with issues and leaders around the world, but also subject them to criticism for going on "junkets" at the taxpayer's expense.

Members of Congress say that the hardest part of their job is being "the prisoner of someone else's schedule." Their staffs have prepared daily schedules for them, broken into fifteen-minute increments, with hearings, meetings, and photo shoots laid out in advance; but at any time, bells can summon them to the chamber to vote, interrupting whatever else they might be doing. After retiring, Senator Paul Laxalt (R-Nevada) commented that what he enjoyed most was "to have a leisurely lunch, to have dinner at home at a reasonable hour, not to have to 'run' to the Senate floor for a vote, not to have your 'schedule card' full of appointments from early morning until late at night."

Regular travel back to their home states means that members spend a lot of time on planes. When Congress lets out, the members can be seen with suit bags over their shoulders sprinting through the concourses of Washington's airports. In the quieter days before the abbreviated Tuesday to Thursday work week, members of the House tried to operate under the rule that political opponents could be friends after 5 p.m., regardless of party. Representative Gene Snyder (R-Kentucky) got backing for a highway bridge in his district during a "happy hour." Snyder regularly played cards with the Democratic Speaker Tip O'Neill in the evening and recalled that after one session, the Speaker put his feet up on Snyder's desk and said, "Gene, you've got your bridge."

As the work week shortened and more congressional families stayed in their home states, members had fewer opportunities to socialize in off-hours—only at prayer breakfasts, workouts in the gymnasium, or an occasional golf match. Even the weekly lunches of the political parties became less social and more partisan, designed to "to game out the issues of the day." Younger members of the House, with fewer responsibilities, will head to the basketball court at the House gymnasium, and those who rush from the showers to the floor to vote get tagged as "wetheads." The Senate offers a health club with exercise machines and a steam bath.

These facilities were once exclusively reserved for men. The House gymnasium, for instance, was built with only a men's locker room, but the sergeant at arms erred in sending invitations to all elected representatives for the grand opening in 1965. When the women members appeared in gym costumes, the men reluctantly made room for them. Women had been elected to Congress since 1917, but the Congressional Caucus for Women's Issues was not founded until 1977. It began with fifteen members. Representative Patricia Schroeder (D-Colorado), who came to the House in 1973, noted that not until some of the senior women members retired could the new generation organize a women's caucus (the older generation had been sensitive about being treated as women as opposed to being treated as members).

As more women won election to Congress and women served on its staff, the dress codes changed. An intrepid House doorkeeper had to remind Representative Bella Abzug (D-New York) that the rules prohibited her from wearing her trademark wide-brimmed hat in the House chamber. The rules did not specifically ban women from wearing slacks or pantsuits, but the men frowned on the practice. Anticipating a Saturday session, when the men tended to dress more casually, women staff in the Senate chamber solicited the support of the women senators serving at the time, and on the appointed Saturday they all dressed in slacks. No objections were raised, and from then on pantsuits or skirts became a matter of individual choice.

The Congressional Black Caucus, created in 1971, tripled in membership during the next three decades, with some of its members going on to attain party leadership posts and chair major committees in the House. Senate elections, being statewide, produce far fewer minority senators. Some states redistricted to promote greater racial and ethnic diversity in the House, drawing district lines that enhanced the chances of Hispanic and African American candidates.

Charles Rangel (D-New York), who chaired the powerful House Ways and Means Committee, pointed out that the "noncompetitive" nature of many of these preponderantly African American districts created safe seats that enabled minority members to accrue seniority and attain committee chairmanships. In many ways, the same dynamics had once allowed white southerners to dominate the House and prevent the passage of civil rights legislation. When those southerners retired or switched parties, they opened the door for minorities to run. The Voting Rights Act of 1965 accelerated this trend by encouraging states to concentrate black voters in "super majority" districts that were more than 65 percent black. Many southern Republicans supported this development because the concentration of Democratic votes in African American districts came at the cost of a net loss of southern Democratic seats in the Congress. In later years, however, some of these black districts saw growth in their Hispanic populations, making them no longer noncompetitive.

Many stalwarts of the Congressional Black Caucus came out of the civil rights movement, where they had led the struggle against an entrenched political establishment. They fought for equal rights and against U.S. support of the apartheid regime in South Africa, and carried those fights into Congress, but they learned that in order to pass legislation they would need to temper their activism through compromise. "If you are around the House long enough, you learn its rules and customs and come to understand that no point of principle is served by remaining a permanent outsider," observed Ron Dellums (D-California), an anti-war activist who became chairman of the House Armed Services Committee. "My constituency, like any other, had sent me to Washington to legislate. I owed them nothing less than my best."

## The staff

The first task for a new member of Congress is to hire a staff and set up an office. Some import their campaign staff from home; others try to hire people who have already acquired experience in the ways of Washington. Either way, the members' staff will be largely populated by politically minded young people, who can rise to positions of responsibility faster in the legislative branch than almost anywhere else. They may start as interns, pages, or congressional fellows, or take jobs in Congress straight from college. They will be required to work long hours for low pay and may burn out after a few years and move on. The more fortunate will join a committee staff, which will enable them to specialize in an issue, earn better pay, and not be subject to the election returns. Usually toiling in anonymity, they devote themselves to advancing their bosses' priorities. "The Hill never stops, and as a young staffer, neither can you," said one in his twenties.

For much of its history, Congress relied on the executive branch departments to generate information and draft legislation and reports. As relations between the executive and legislative branches became strained during the twentieth century, however, Congress sought more independent sources of data and assistance. In 1914, during the Progressive era, it created the Legislative Reference Service in the Library of Congress, which later expanded into the Congressional Research Service, to provide politically neutral issue briefs and lend staff to augment the support network for members and committees. Other legislative branch agencies include the Congressional Budget Office, which provides a reality check for the budget information that Congress receives from the executive branch, and the Government Accountability Office (formerly the General Accounting Office), which investigates how the executive branch implements the laws and spends the funds Congress appropriates. Also part of the legislative branch is the Government Printing Office, which produces the *Congressional Record* and a host of other government publications.

The Legislative Reorganization Act of 1946 established the first professional staffs for committees and also allowed members to expand their personal staffs. Each member could employ an administrative assistant to supervise the staff, and legislative assistants to handle specific areas of legislation, researching, drafting, and tracking bills to keep the member informed about them. Members also appoint staff to the committees on which they serve, to attend meetings that members might miss, to negotiate amendments with other staff, as well as to advise the members on pending votes. These staff members have been called "unelected lawmakers" and "virtual senators." Near the end of his forty-seven years in the Senate, Ted Kennedy observed that " 95 percent of the nitty-gritty work" of drafting and negotiating bills was being done by staff. But a certificate of election still separates them from those who hold the ultimate power and authority.

Relationships between members and their staff vary according to individual style, reflecting the daily pressures of the job and the aggressive personalities that got them elected in the first place. Some legislators are beloved by loyal staff; others are feared. Some can retain staff for years, while others experience constant turnover. A famous abuser of his staff was Lyndon Johnson (D-Texas), who could humiliate those who worked for him in public but still manage to hold their loyalty, because he always pushed himself as hard as he pushed them. Senators and representatives receive office allowances to spend as they see fit, within limits. They may hire fewer aides at higher salaries to maintain stability or employ a larger staff at less pay. Younger staffers take these demanding positions to gain a few years of congressional experience to use as a stepping stool to better paying positions inside and outside the government.

The mounting legislative workload and flood of constituent mail accounted for the growth of the congressional staff. In 1908 and 1909 the House and Senate opened their first office buildings, on the south and north sides of the Capitol, respectively. The office buildings provided space for more public hearings, more staff, and more opportunity for members to meet with constituents. The first House Office Building, later named for Speaker Joseph Cannon, was designed in a classical style that complemented the Capitol. It originally had 397 offices, one room per member and fourteen committee rooms, connected by tunnel to the Capitol. A second House office building, named for Speaker Nicholas Longworth (R-Ohio), was completed in 1933, and a third, named for Speaker Sam Rayburn, opened in 1965, provided suites of rooms for each member's growing staff.

The first Senate Office Building (known by its unfortunate acronym SOB), later named for Richard Russell, adopted the same exterior design as the House office building, but since it served fewer members had a more spacious and elegant interior. Wooden mantles in the House offices became marble in the

Senate offices; iron railings became brass; veneer became solid mahogany. Senate offices initially consisted of two rooms, one for the senator, the other for his staff. A second SOB was added in 1958, named for Senator Everett M. Dirksen (R-Illinois), and a third in 1983, named for Senator Philip Hart (D-Michigan). With each addition, the number of rooms assigned to each senator increased dramatically. A typical office today connects space that would once have housed a half-dozen senators and their staff.

Located across the street from the Capitol, the House and Senate office buildings required members to shuttle back and forth repeatedly from their offices to the chamber to vote. In the 1890s, Thomas Edison had overseen the wiring of the Capitol for electricity and had installed bells to summon the members to vote. In 1912 the Senate installed the first electric subway cars between its office building and the Capitol, operating as a horizontal elevator. Like a school changing classes, the sound of a long bell, signaling a vote, brings a sudden rush of senators from their offices and committee rooms to the subway. Senator Norris Cotton (R-New Hampshire) relished the story of a new page escorting an elderly woman into the galleries. She demanded to know why so many bells were ringing. "I'm not quite sure," replied the page "…maybe one of them has escaped."

## Lobbyists and other visitors

Besides members and staff, other regulars on Capitol Hill include lobbyists and journalists. The term lobbyist—sometimes prefaced as "K Street lobbyists" because of the high concentration of their offices on that street—has become associated with special interests and questionable backroom dealings, yet lobbyists are a legitimate part of the legislative process. In the era of torchlight parades and intense electoral competition, nineteenth-century legislators took their cues largely from their parties. Voter turnout peaked in 1896 and began a long slide in the twentieth century, when citizens began seeking more direct ways to influence legislators by organizing into private interest groups. These groups provided information that legislators used both for drafting laws and for running for reelection.

Lobbyists know Congress, sometimes having served as legislators or congressional staff, and can offer expertise in specific issues. They may represent corporations, labor unions, local governments, universities, teachers, hospitals, veterans, farmers, ranchers, oil and gas producers, consumers, and a myriad of other groups. Some are better funded than others, but they all have played an increasingly prominent role in raising campaign funds for members running for reelection, which in turn has expanded their influence over the legislators and legislation. It is a truism that those who contribute get the ear of the member and the staff, said Representative Roman Mazzoli (D-Kentucky). "They have the access and access is it. Access is power. Access is clout."

Lobbyists have an "Iron Triangle" theory that their chance of legislative success is greatest when three factors are in play: they have chairs of the pertinent committees on their side; they have high-level officials within the relevant executive agency interested in enacting and implementing the issue; and they have a strong constituency they can mobilize for it on the outside. Lobbyists will also provide members and staff with detailed background information and establish contacts with leaders in the field being legislated, to keep Congress abreast of what one lobbyist has called "economic and political realities."

The money spent on Washington lobbying has reached billions of dollars a year, and the number of lobbyists has grown to thousands. In 2006, a lobbying scandal erupted around Jack Abramoff, who represented a number of Indian tribes that were anxious to prevent Congress from imposing a tax on the revenues of Indian gambling casinos. Abramoff courted key members of Congress and the administration by paying their expenses for golfing trips to Scotland, entertaining them in skyboxes at sports events, and funneling funds into their campaigns in return for their legislative support. He charged his clients exorbitant fees for his high-level access. The government investigated, and Abramoff pleaded guilty to fraud and tax evasion. Association with him cost several members their elections and prompted Congress to tighten restrictions on what lobbyists could legitimately do.

Members insist that the most effective lobbyists are "the ones back home." But few issues before Congress register strongly enough for citizens to voice much of an opinion, and pollsters say it is hard to test a wind that is not blowing. If the public seems unconcerned, lobbyists will try to generate their own grassroots campaigns, which legislators dismiss as "astroturf" lobbying for their artificial nature. Members realize that lobbyists are "hired guns," paid to support or oppose something by orchestrating publicity and meetings with members of Congress. But they must work with outside groups and interests in order to construct workable public policy. Hearing from a variety of these groups, through their lobbyists, helps those writing the laws to understand the likely consequences and to adjust bills to avoid disasters.

Although some members of Congress campaign for reelection by "running against Washington," a lot of them stay when they retire, a condition ascribed to "Potomac Fever." Many members have spent the largest share of their adult years in the capital and have developed knowledge and skills that enable them to operate more effectively there than back home. One study calculated that from 1998 to 2004, 43 percent of all retired members of Congress engaged in lobbying, as did their senior staff. Ethics reforms have banned them from lobbying Congress for two years after they leave office, but they spend the requisite cooling off period consulting rather than doing any direct lobbying. Lobbying disclosure rules also require that those who contact members of Congress for the purpose of influencing legislation must file public reports on who hired them, what they were paid, and what contributions they made to public officials.

Former members who become lobbyists enjoy an open-door policy with their old friends in Congress, although they find that their congressional friends will have their hands out for campaign contributions. Such contributions are regarded as an investment to spend more time with their clients' representatives "in a less formal setting," as one defense lobbyist explained. To this end, lobby groups organize fund-raising events for members' reelection campaigns. Lobbyists often seek members' help in obtaining earmarked funds for projects in their home state, which the members can then cite as accomplishments during their reelection campaigns, a further advantage for incumbents.

Among the lobbyists are squads of liaisons for government agencies and the military services. They guide the top brass through the Congress, helping to prepare their testimony and collecting information to respond to questions they could not answer. Military liaisons are responsible for answering thousands of constituent inquiries routed to them by members of Congress, often involving transfers, awards, and pay issues. Liaison officers will accompany members on fact-finding missions, even escorting them into war zones. Above all, their job is to maintain good relations with Congress so that their branch of the service can maintain adequate appropriations.

Others who sport congressional identification badges are the army of reporters, broadcasters, and photographers who operate out of the press galleries. Their IDs enable them to gather in the corridors to interview members as they emerge from meetings or head to the chambers to vote. Some reporters are stationed regularly at the Capitol, where they develop deep knowledge of its operations, although their need to cultivate regular sources at times compromises their ability to write candidly about those sources. Other reporters come to the Hill only when some news is breaking and thus can be more independent, but their grasp of the institution may be less solid. Anxious for good press, senators and representatives hire experienced journalists to serve as their press secretaries, facilitating relations with the press corps. Members of Congress consume great quantities of information in print, on the air, including three privately published trade papers that are distributed to all congressional offices: *Roll Call*, *The Hill*, and *Politico*. The issue-oriented *Congress Daily* and *National Journal* are also followed closely by members and staff.

Fellowships constitute yet another component of the Hill community. Since 1953 the American Political Science Association has run an annual congressional fellowship program that sends political scientists, journalists, doctors, and international scholars into House and Senate offices to gain hands-on understanding of the legislative process as members of the congressional staff. The APSA's most prominent alumnus, Dick Cheney, came to Washington as a fellow in 1968. He established connections with Representative Donald Rumsfeld (R-Illinois), who helped him within seven years catapult into the position of White House chief of staff. Cheney went on to serve as a representative, secretary of defense, and vice president of the United States, but he never returned to the University of Wisconsin to complete his doctorate. The Congressional Black Caucus sponsors a fellowship program that encourages the hiring of more African Americans as staff in Congress. The Women's Research and Education Institute gives fellowships to men and women to spend a year on the congressional staff working on policy issues affecting women. Scientists and engineers can get fellowships from the American Association for the Advancement of Science (AAAS) to provide their scientific expertise to the policy-making processes. The American Psychological Association (APA) recruits fellows to promote more effective use of psychological knowledge in government. Faculty have used their sabbaticals to work as congressional fellows, drafted legislation, gotten caught up in the legislative and political currents, and wound up staying for decades on Capitol Hill as influential members of the staff.

Some scholars also run for Congress. David Price (D-North Carolina) had spent twenty years as a professor of political science at Duke University and had written several books on Congress before he was elected to a House seat (his television ad featured him in a classroom). He found that his years of teaching, and his summer internships on the Hill, helped prepare him for the uncommon demands of the job. Although given committee assignments appropriate to his state, Price had studied and written about congressional committees long enough to set his sights on the Appropriations Committee, whose control of funds gave it "far more power than any other committee." A prominent academic on the Senate side was Daniel Patrick Moynihan (D-New York), who earned a Ph.D. in sociology and directed the Joint Center for Urban Studies at Harvard University and the Massachusetts Institute of Technology before going on to serve three terms in the Senate and chairing the Finance Committee.

Then there are the vast numbers of daily visitors from across the nation and around the globe. On average, American citizens visit the U.S. Capitol twice in their lives, once as children with their families or with their classes, and again as parents, bringing their own families. As late as the 1970s, citizens could enter and wander through the Capitol at will whenever Congress was in session, with almost no restrictions. Bombings in the Capitol by radical groups in 1971 and 1983, the killing of two Capitol Police by a deranged gunman in 1998, and the terrorist threats of 2001 all heightened security considerably, with metal detectors installed at all entrances and some sections of the building made off-limits to those without official badges. Yet the Capitol has stayed more accessible to the public than most other government offices. Visitors are encouraged, since they are constituents and voters. Sunshine rules require committees to open their hearings to the public, and members' offices provide constituents with free tickets for the Senate and House galleries. By the end of the twentieth century, more than three million people a year were visiting the Capitol.

To handle the crowds, a vast underground Capitol Visitor Center was constructed beneath the East Front plaza. In its Emancipation Hall stands the nineteen-foot plaster model for the bronze statue of Freedom. Waiting to tour the Capitol, visitors can examine a museum devoted to the history of the Senate, the House, and the Capitol, and view an orientation film. Through skylights they can glance up at the Capitol dome, the most recognizable symbol of American representative democracy.

"Congress isn't perfect," a *Washington Post* editorial pronounced at the opening of the visitor center in 2008. "Grand displays of courage by its 535 members aren't as frequent as we would like. But the complex they so generously funded does honor to a history of accomplishment whose impact reaches far beyond Capitol Hill." The notion of displaying courage usually involves defying public opinion, a characteristic that made Philip Hart (D-Michigan) known as the "conscience of the Senate." Hart sponsored stricter handgun laws, despite a large percentage of gun owners and hunters in his state, and fought Michigan's predominant industry, car manufacturers, on antitrust matters. Yet it is a fundamental paradox of Congress that its members are elected to promote their constituent's concerns, and when they do, they can be criticized for parochialism. When they stand against public opinion, they risk their seats. Individually concerned with reelection and the interests of their districts and states, collectively they must fuse those local concerns into national legislation, finding common ground for the common good, and fulfilling the motto *E Pluribus Unum*.

# Further reading

Congress publishes most of what it does, including the full text of its debates in the daily *Congressional Record*, most of its public hearings, reports, and other documents. The Congressional Information Service has microfilmed and indexed the hearings and reports, by committee, subject, and witness. This information can be found in the government documents sections of larger libraries, and much of it is also online at http://thomas.loc.gov/. *Thomas* is a legislative information site provided by the Library of Congress, where researchers can browse and search full text of bills and debates since 1995. Its related site, *A Century of Lawmaking for a New Nation, lcweb2.loc.gov/ammem/amlaw/*, includes all published congressional documents from the Continental Congress in 1774 through the U.S. Congress in 1875.

The subscription services Lexis-Nexis and Heine Online have created databases that will allow full-text searching of the *Congressional Record* and all hearings, reports, and related documents. The Government Printing Office (GPO) also makes all recent congressional publications available at www.gpoaccess.gov/serialset/cdocuments/featured/senate.html. The original documents, and the unpublished records of Congress, are located in Record Groups 46 (Senate), 128 (Joint Committees), and 233 (House) in the Center for Legislative Archives of the National Archives and Records Administration, Washington, D.C.

Web sites for the U.S. Senate (www.senate.gov) and House of Representatives (www.clerk.house.gov) provide information on the current committees and members of Congress, along with copious historical information and reference materials. An important feature of the Senate Web site is the text of two volumes of Senator Robert C. Byrd's *The Senate, 1789-1989: Addresses on the History of the United States Senate* (Washington, D.C.: Government Printing Office, 1988 and 1991). The site also contains full transcripts of oral history interviews with senators, and Senate staff. The House Clerk's Web site includes material from its reference books *Black Americans in Congress, 1870-2007* and *Women in Congress, 1917-2006*. Both Web sites also feature the *Biographical Directory of the U.S. Congress*, with brief biographies of every member, together with bibliographies and research collections regarding their careers. The Association of Centers for the Study of Congress (ACSC), at www.congresscenters.org/index .htm, is an independent alliance of organizations and institutions that promote the study of the U.S. Congress and house the papers of its former members. Other information and live and archived broadcasts from the House and Senate can be accessed at C-SPAN Online: www.cspan.org.

The privately published *Congressional Quarterly (CQ)* produces an abundance of handy publications, including *CQ Daily*, *CQ Almanac*, *Guide to Congress*, *Congress and the Nation*, and *Landmark Documents on the U.S. Congress*, many of which are available online as well as in print. Other essential reference volumes are Donald C. Bacon, Richard H. Davidson, and Morton Keller, eds., *The Encyclopedia of the United States Congress*, 4 vols. (New York: Simon & Schuster, 1995); and Norman J. Ornstein, Thomas E. Mann, and Michael J. Malbin, *Vital Statistics on Congress* (Washington, D.C.: American Enterprise Institute, 2002).

## Selected books about Congress

Baker, Richard A., and Roger A. Davidson, eds. *First Among Equals: Outstanding Senate Leaders of the Twentieth Century*. Washington, D.C.: CQ Press, 1991.

Baker, Ross K. *House and Senate*. 4th ed. New York: W. W. Norton, 2008.

Bowling, Kenneth R., and Donald R. Kennon, eds. *Inventing Congress: Origins and Establishment of the First Federal Congress*. Athens: Ohio University Press, 1999.

Brown, Sherrod. *Congress from the Inside: Observations from the Majority and the Minority*. 3rd ed. Kent, Ohio: Kent State University Press, 2004.

Bzdek, Vincent. *Woman of the House: The Rise of Nancy Pelosi*. New York: Palgrave/Macmillan, 2008.

Campbell, Karl E. *Senator Sam Ervin, Last of the Founding Fathers*. Chapel Hill: University of North Carolina Press, 2007.

Caro, Robert A. *The Years of Lyndon Johnson: The Path to Power, Means of Assent, and Master of the Senate*. New York: Knopf, 1982–2002.

Davidson, Roger H., Susan Webb Hammond, and Raymond W. Smock, eds. *Masters of the House: Congressional Leadership Over Two Centuries*. New York: Westview, 1998.

Davidson, Roger H., and Walter J. Oleszek. *Congress and Its Members*. 10th ed. Washington, D.C.: CQ Press, 2006.

Dodd, Lawrence C., and Bruce I. Oppenheimer. *Congress Reconsidered*. 9th ed. Washington, D.C.: CQ Press, 2009.

Doherty, Thomas. *Cold War, Cool Medium: Television, McCarthyism and American Culture*. New York: Columbia University Press, 2003.

Fenno, Richard F., Jr. *Congressional Travels: Places, Connections, and Authenticity*. New York: Pearson/Longman, 2007.

———. *Home Style: House Members in Their Districts*. New York: Little, Brown, 1978.

Freeman, Joanne. *Affairs of Honor: National Politics in the New Republic*. New Haven, Conn.: Yale University Press, 2002.

Frey, Lou Jr., and Michael T. Hayes. *Inside the House: Former Members Reveal How Congress Really Works*. Lanham, Md.: University Press of America, 2001.

Gertzog, Irwin. *Women and Power on Capitol Hill: Reconstructing the Congressional Women's Caucus*. Boulder, Colo.: Lynne Rienner, 2004.

Gillon, Steven M. *The Pact: Bill Clinton, Newt Gingrich, and the Rivalry that Defined a Generation*. New York: Oxford University Press, 2008.

Hansen, John Mark. *Gaining Access: Congress and the Farm Lobby, 1919–1981*. Chicago: University of Chicago Press, 1991.

Howell, William G., and John C. Pevehouse. *While Dangers Gather: Congressional Checks on Presidential War Power*. Princeton, N.J.: Princeton University Press, 2007.

Jacobs, John. *A Rage for Justice: The Passion and Politics of Phillip Burton*. Berkeley: University of California Press, 1995.

Johnson, Robert David. *Congress and the Cold War*. New York: Cambridge University Press, 2006.

Kaufman, Robert G. *Henry M. Jackson: A Life in Politics*. Seattle: University of Washington Press, 2000.

Killian, Linda. *The Freshmen: What Happened to the Republican Revolution?* Boulder, Colo.: Westview, 1998.

Kyvig, David E. *The Age of Impeachment: American Constitutional Culture Since 1960*. Lawrence: University Press of Kansas, 2008.

Mann, Thomas E., and Norman J. Ornstein. *The Broken Branch: How Congress Is Failing America and How to Get It Back on Track*. New York: Oxford University Press, 2006.

Martis, Kenneth C. *The Historical Atlas of Political Parties in the United States Congress, 1789–1989*. New York: Macmillan, 1989.

Mayhew, David R. *America's Congress: Actions in the Public Sphere, James Madison through Newt Gingrich*. New Haven, Conn.: Yale University Press, 2000.

——— . *Congress: The Electoral Connection*. 2nd ed. New Haven, Conn.: Yale University Press, 2004.

——— . *Divided We Govern: Party Control, Law Making, and Investigation, 1946–2002*. 2nd ed. New Haven, Conn.: Yale University Press, 2005.

Milazzo, Paul Charles. *Unlikely Environmentalists: Congress and Clean Water, 1945–1972*. Lawrence: University Press of Kansas, 2006.

Panagopoulos, Costas, and Joshua Schank. *All Roads Lead to Congress: The $300 Billion Fight over Highway Funding*. Washington, D.C.: CQ Press, 2008.

Patterson, Kelly D., and Daniel M. Shea, eds. *Contemplating the People's Branch: Legislative Dynamics in the Twenty-First Century*. Saddle River, N.J.: Prentice Hall, 2000.

Polsby, Nelson W. *How Congress Evolves: Social Bases of Institutional Change*. New York: Oxford University Press, 2004.

Power, Timothy J., and Nicol C. Rae, eds. *Exporting Congress? The Influence of the U.S. Congress on World Legislatures*. Pittsburgh: University of Pittsburgh Press, 2006.

Price, David E. *The Congressional Experience: A View from the Hill*. Boulder, Colo.: Westview, 1992.

Quirk, Paul J., and Sarah A. Binder, eds. *The Legislative Branch*. New York: Oxford University Press, 2005.

Redman, Eric. *The Dance of Legislation*. Seattle: University of Washington Press, 2001.

Remini, Robert V. *Daniel Webster: The Man and His Time*. New York: W. W. Norton, 1997.

——— . *Henry Clay: Statesman for the Union*. New York: W. W. Norton, 1991.

——— . *The House: The History of the House of Representatives*. New York: HarperCollins, 2006.

Ritchie, Donald A. *The Congress of the United States: A Student Companion*. 3rd ed. New York: Oxford University Press, 2006.

——— . *Press Gallery: Congress and the Washington Correspondents*. Cambridge, Mass.: Harvard University Press, 1991.

Sinclair, Barbara. *Unorthodox Lawmaking: New Legislative Processes in the U.S. Congress*. Washington, D.C.: CQ Press, 2007.

Smith, Steven S., Jason M. Roberts, and Ryan J. Vander Wielen. *The American Congress*. New York: Cambridge University Press, 2006.

Strahan, Randall. *Leading Representatives: The Agency of Leaders in the Politics of the U.S. House*. Baltimore, Md.: Johns Hopkins University Press, 2007.

Woods, Randall. *Fulbright: A Biography*. New York: Cambridge University Press, 2006.

Zelizer, Julian E., ed. *The American Congress: The Building of Democracy*. Boston: Houghton Mifflin, 2004.

——— . *On Capitol Hill: The Struggle to Reform Congress and its Consequences, 1948–2000*. New York: Cambridge University Press, 2006.

——— . *Taxing America: Wilbur D. Mills, Congress, and the State, 1945–1975*. New York: Cambridge University Press, 1998.

## Notable films on Congress

*Advise and Consent* (1962): From a novel based loosely on actual events, the movie was shot on Capitol Hill, using real senators, staff, and reporters as extras.

*Charlie Wilson's War* (2007): A film version of the exploits of a congressman who used the legislative process to fund the mujahideen against the Soviet military in Afghanistan.

*The Congress* (1988): Ken Burns's documentary celebrated the congressional bicentennial.

*Mr. Smith Goes to Washington* (1939): The classic Hollywood version of a Senate filibuster.

*Point of Order* (1964) and *Good Night and Good Luck* (2005): The corrosive effects of Senator Joseph McCarthy's anti-Communist investigations are revealed in a documentary and film.

# Index

## N

## O

## P

# THE AMERICAN PRESIDENCY
## A Very Short Introduction
Charles O. Jones

This marvelously concise survey is packed with information about the American presidency. Charles O. Jones explores the rise of federal power and the dramatic expansion of federal agencies, showing how the president takes a direct hand in this vast bureaucracy, and he examines the political process of selecting presidents, from the days of deadlocked conventions to the rise of the primary after World War II.

"In 200 years," he writes, "the presidency had changed from that of a person—Washington followed by Adams, then Jefferson—to a presidential enterprise with a cast of thousands." Jones explains how this remarkable expansion has occurred and where it may lead in the future.

> "This crisp and succinct book provides a superb introduction to the American presidency for students and general readers and can be read with profit and pleasure by specialists. I recommend it wholeheartedly."
>
> **Fred I. Greenstein, Professor of Politics Emeritus,**
> **Princeton University**

www.oup.com/uk/isbn/978-0-19-530701-6

# AMERICAN POLITICAL PARTIES AND ELECTIONS
## A Very Short Introduction
L. Sandy Maisel

Participation in elections in the United States is much lower than in the vast majority of mature democracies. Perhaps this is because of the lack of competition in a country where only two parties have a true chance of winning. Or perhaps it is because, in the United States, campaign contributions disproportionately favor incumbents in most legislative elections. This Very Short Introduction introduces the reader to these issues and more, providing an insider's view of how the system actually works while shining a light on some of its flaws. It offers readers a very clear picture indeed of the problems that underlie America's electoral system.

> "For anyone who really wants to understand our election system, and the role of the political parties that are at its core, this book is absolutely indispensable."
>
> **Mickey Edwards, Princeton University;**
> **former U.S. congressman**

www.oup.com/uk/isbn/978-0-19-530122-9

# PROGRESSIVISM
## A Very Short Introduction
Walter Nugent

This very timely Very Short Introduction offers an engaging overview of Progressivism in America—its origins, guiding principles, major leaders and major accomplishments. A many-sided reform movement that lasted from the late 1890s until the early 1920s, Progressivism emerged as a response to the excesses of the Gilded Age, an era that plunged working Americans into poverty while a new class of ostentatious millionaires built huge mansions and flaunted their wealth. Nugent shows that the Progressives—with the glaring exception of race relations—shared a common conviction that society should be fair to all its members and that governments had a responsibility to see that fairness prevailed.

Offering a succinct history of the broad reform movement that upset a stagnant conservative orthodoxy, this Very Short Introduction reveals many parallels, even lessons, highly appropriate to our own time.

> "Nugent's elegant treatment is not only a masterful synthesis of the field, it is an important interpretive intervention that will inspire the continued rethinking of the chronology and the politics—as well as the many virtues—of the Progressives."
>
> **Robert D. Johnston, author of *The Radical Middle Class: Populist Democracy and the Question of Capitalism in Progressive Era Portland, Oregon***

www.oup.com/uk/isbn/978-0-19-531106-8

# THE GREAT DEPRESSION AND THE NEW DEAL
## A Very Short Introduction
Eric Rauchway

In this superb compact history, Eric Rauchway offers an informed account of the Great Depression and the New Deal. Rauchway first describes how the roots of the Great Depression lay in America's post-war economic policies that in effect isolated our nation from the world economy just when the world needed the United States most. He then introduces the concept of the New Deal, illustrating the many programs it involved, ranging from the National Recovery Agency and the Securities and Exchange Commission to the Public Works Administration and Social Security, and revealing why some worked and others did not.

The New Deal shaped our nation's politics for decades and was seen by many as tantamount to the "American Way" itself. Today we can look back and, for the first time, see its full complexity. Rauchway captures this complexity in a remarkably short space, making this book an ideal introduction to one of the great policy revolutions in history.

> "This book is the place where everyone should start in trying to understand the Depression and the efforts of the New Deal to get the United States back to prosperity. It is insightful, thought-provoking, and relevant to uncertain economic times."
>
> **John Milton Cooper, Jr., University of Wisconsin-Madison**

www.oup.com/uk/isbn/978-0-19-532634-5